EUROPEAN MEMORIES

First Published in Great Britain 2021 by Mirador Publishing

First edition: 2021

This book is taken from the memories of the author. References to places and people are made with due respect. Any offence caused by references in the narrative is completely unintentional.

A copy of this work is available through the British Library.

ISBN: 978-1-913833-88-6

Mirador Publishing
10 Greenbrook Terrace
Taunton
Somerset
UK
TA1 1UT

EUROPEAN MEMORIES

ROSEMARY LEE

Contents

Bosnia coffee

Introduction

WE ALL KNOW EUROPE, DON'T we? After all, Britain is part of Europe – at least geographically, if no longer politically. Yet this is such a varied continent, with a huge range of landscapes and centuries of history, which both links and divides its countries and regions – can anyone claim to know it intimately? And it is constantly evolving … areas which we once knew well, seem changed out of all recognition when we return decades, or even a few years later. I have been exploring Europe for over 50 years – my earliest experiences came when I was still young and naive, travelling with tight constraints on my budget; later there were exploratory solo trips by car to some of the lesser-known corners of the continent, and visits to friends in various countries; in recent years, I have even joined some escorted tours, benefiting from the knowledge of professional guides. However, many of my memories come from the 25 years I spent as a tour manager, leading coachloads of up to 50 passengers at a time, around the principal sights of Europe.

For over 5 years (1975-80) I worked for a budget company, operating fast-moving tours, staying in basic accommodation and often 'flying by the seat of my pants' as I learned my trade – many of my most outrageous memories date from this period. In the 1980s and 90s, I moved to a company offering higher quality tours, often with time to explore some more off-the-beaten-track destinations – though every guest still wanted to see the most famous sights as well, since they were the places their friends had talked about. As I became more experienced, I began to specialise in tours behind the Iron Curtain, with all the technical challenges they brought. Later I found myself often leading my company's longest trips, travelling from one end of Europe to the other, on tours lasting 25 or even 36 days. Many of my colleagues did not like these long tours, but I enjoyed the chance to mould each group into a supportive 'family', and to give my guests a comprehensive insight into the similarities and differences between countries throughout the continent.

In the late 1990s I began to spend part of the off-season, teaching tourism to 16-18-year-old students, until (in 2000) I ceased working as a tour manager altogether to concentrate on teaching. However, there were still opportunities to lead groups into Europe – this time groups of students, with all the extra responsibilities involved in supervising young people as they enjoyed their first taste of travelling abroad. I was delighted to be able to introduce them to new experiences, though sometimes found it difficult to match their interests with the sights I wanted to show them.

When I started to write this book, I was convinced that I had forgotten much of what I had seen and experienced – yet the more I wrote, the more I remembered, till I was wallowing in memories like a hippo in a mud bath! I found myself recalling snippets of the commentary which I gave my guests to help them understand the places they were visiting, especially the historical situations which allowed the building of important architectural highlights – and also some of the European tales and legends which entertained them along the way. Images of my favourite locations floated again through my mind, together with the places most enjoyed by my guests – stunning buildings, awe-inspiring scenery and unforgettable activities. Memories of situations and events, some challenging and some (with the benefit of hindsight) humorous, flowed on to the page. All of this, I have tried to record into this memoir.

Come and travel with me through the countries of Europe, as I have known them!

Russia - Street entertainer

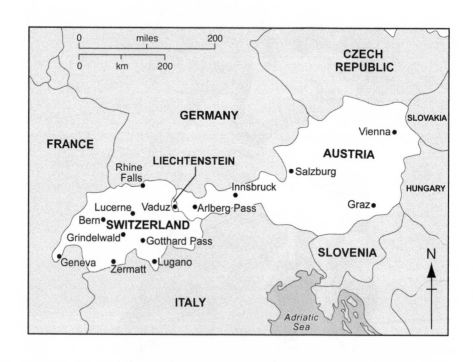

THE ALPINE LANDS

SWITZERLAND

I HAVE ALWAYS LOVED MOUNTAINS, so what better place to start this tour of my European memories, than amid Europe's most impressive mountain range, the Alps ... and in the country which is 60% covered by these mountains: Switzerland. When I first started escorting tours through the country, the main road to Italy still climbed up tight bends to the treeless heights of the Gotthard Pass at 2106m (almost 7000ft), but the summits of both the Grand St Bernard Pass (where the dogs come from) and the San Bernardino Pass had already been tunnelled through in the 1960s. However, in 1980 our journey across the Gotthard was transformed by the opening of a 17km (10½ mi) road tunnel beneath the Pass – an engineering marvel which made our journey much smoother and quicker, but sadly meant that my guests lost an opportunity to enjoy the majesty of the mountains. And of course, there was the problem of claustrophobia – one of my guests was so affected as the tunnel went on ... and on ... and on, that she was hyperventilating by the time we emerged, and we had to make an unscheduled roadside stop for her to suck in some fresh air and compose herself again. In 2016, Switzerland opened a new rail tunnel beneath the Gotthard Pass, currently longest in the world at 57km (35½ mi), easing the journey of transiting trucks but, in my eyes, also losing another chance to marvel at magnificent alpine scenery – I doubt I will be using it! Yet the old roads across the passes are still in existence and are still negotiable in the summer months. When I started teaching and could travel in high summer,

I took the opportunity to rent a car and drive across some of them – most notably the Albula Pass (2312m/ 7500ft), where I was almost alone with the cattle grazing on open, airy pastures amid rocky peaks, and the Susten Pass (2259m/ 7400ft) with fabulous views back over the Stein Glacier.

Springtime in the high mountains was always a special treat – Swiss farmers use only 'natural fertiliser' (provided from the rear of their cows!) on the meadows, so the wild flowers bloom in abundance. On one occasion, travelling in early May when the snow was only just melting away from the high pastures, I was lucky enough to see marmots just waking from their winter hibernation – furry noses suddenly appearing from otherwise untouched expanses of snow, and often we saw them scurrying across the hillsides in high summer, whistling frantically to warn the rest of their colony of potential danger from hawks in the skies above them. Everywhere we saw herds of Swiss Brown cows, with the most beautiful eyelashes you will ever see on a cow! Towards the end of summer, we sometimes saw the cattle being brought down to the villages from their summer pasture, escorted by herdsmen and women dressed in the embroidered jackets or long skirts and aprons of their national costume. The cattle themselves are decorated with head-dresses of flowers and huge bells hanging from leather collars around their necks – the noise as they pass is almost deafening, though the cows do not seem to be worried by it (perhaps because they wear smaller bells all summer, so that the herdsmen can track their location on the summer pastures). The herds fill the road, meandering along at a leisurely pace, brushing up against the coach as they pass, only occasionally turning off towards an especially juicy patch of grazing and needing to be turned again by the herders. What mayhem inside the coach at the sight, with all the photographers climbing over each other in an attempt to get the best shot!

Because of the difficult terrain, with many valleys and regions virtually cut off from their neighbours, Switzerland has a decentralised form of government – it is a federation of states (cantons) which largely run their own affairs, with a national government concerned mainly with external affairs, based in the small city of Bern. Despite being in the heart of Europe, the Swiss have decided not to join the EU (though they have special trading arrangements with it), and they also manage their own national defence. They have managed to remain neutral throughout all the wars of the past centuries (not fighting outside their own borders since the 16th century), but it is an armed neutrality – virtually the entire male population goes for regular military training so that they can protect their own part of the country if necessary. Though it is a small country, just 17% the size of the UK, it is home to a variety of peoples and languages – 63% speak Swiss German, 30% (in the far west) speak French, 10% (in the south) speak Italian, and in a few areas of eastern Switzerland they speak Romansch.

Virtually all of the European tours which I escorted, concentrated their Swiss sightseeing on the German-speaking parts of the country, especially the picturesque town of Lucerne. It is located just at the point where Lake Lucerne flows out into the River Reuss, passing beneath two covered wooden bridges with splendid paintings decorating the inside of their roofs – I always recommended my guests to walk slowly over the bridges to see those paintings, though as the years passed and Lucerne became ever busier, it was sometimes impossible to walk across because of the crowds. Lucerne's location on the shores of its lake is so pretty that my guests were always enchanted by the town, though they were rather taken aback by the unsmiling service they received in our hotels – always faultlessly efficient but lacking in any trace of friendliness. All around Europe, I taught my guests a greeting in each local language (in German-speaking Switzerland, it was 'Greutzi') but when they enthusiastically tried it out at the hotel in Lucerne, the tight-laced receptionist assumed only that they were mocking her language and became angry! At least there was some relaxed humour when we attended a folklore dinner and show in the city's casino building – fun as guests attempted to dip cubes of bread on forks into boiling cheese fondue, without dropping them (the penalty was kissing the person next to them on the table), and a jovial host who introduced the folk dances, alpine horns and bellringers with hilarious comments which seemed to my guests to be off-the-cuff. However, since I attended hundreds of the shows, I quickly realised that his patter was identical on every occasion, though delivered with consummate Swiss professionalism which made it seem fresh every time.

Highlight of our visit was usually an ascent of one of the nearby mountains. Mount Pilatus (2125m/ 6900ft) made an interesting visit because we ascended on the world's steepest cogwheel railway and descended on a cable car, but the mountain itself is simply a rocky peak with a viewing platform. When possible, I preferred to take my guests to Mount Titlis (3238m/ 10600ft), taking two cable cars (one being the world's first revolving cable car, opened in 1992) to find guaranteed snow to play in at the top. For some of my Australian guests (as well as those from Malaysia and Singapore), this was the first time they had ever seen snow – they leapt and frolicked with such enthusiasm that some succumbed to the effects of altitude and had to sit down to catch their breath, or even turn tail and descend the mountain again. The summit is covered by a glacier, with a tunnel carved into it so that it is possible to actually walk through the illuminated ice: I always tried to enter the tunnel when there was no-one else around and it was possible to hear the ice creaking as it moved slowly around me. Since the days when I brought groups here, the management of the Titlis facilities has added other attractions – a slope where tourists can slide down on inner tubes (I am sure today's tour managers are having to cope with a flurry of minor injuries), and a hanging metal bridge (the Cliff Walk) opened in 2012 and now the highest altitude, suspended bridge in Europe. Tourism never stands still!

When I first started bringing guests to this area in the 1970s, we travelled along the length of Lake Lucerne (properly called Vierwaldstädtersee) using the original road, including the stretch known as the Axenstrasse, which clung to the cliffs beside the water, in places travelling through narrow and dark tunnels, barely large enough for the coach – often we had to stop and manoeuvre our way past oncoming vehicles. Today the old road has been abandoned by traffic, used only by cyclists and hikers, while a new wider road and straighter tunnels have been built higher up the cliff. Even this new road is still often threatened by rockfalls, and in 2020 an alarm system was installed: triggered by the vibration of falling rocks, it automatically closes the road (with traffic lights) until the danger has been investigated. The tunnels on the old road are equipped with rock-cut windows looking out over the lake – from one window, I could point out William Tell's chapel, which gave me the chance to tell my guests the story of Switzerland's national hero. Throughout my career as a tour manager, I collected folk tales to recount to my guests as we passed through the appropriate regions, and by the time we reached Switzerland, they were waiting to enjoy their 'story time':

"Long ago, when Switzerland was still ruled by the Austrian Habsburg emperors, this region was governed by a cruel and arrogant man named Gessler. He erected a pole in the middle of the village of Altdorf (beside Lake Lucerne) and hung his hat from the top, announcing that everyone who passed must bow to the hat, as a sign of respect for the emperor. One day, William Tell (a local farmer) came into the village with his son – he refused to bow to the hat and declared he would not even bow to the emperor himself. He was seized by soldiers and taken to Gessler, who offered to let Tell go free if he could shoot an apple from the head of his own son (Tell was famous for his skill with a crossbow). The shot was accurate, but Gessler was scared by this evidence of Tell's skill and arrested him, putting him in chains into a small boat to cross Lake Lucerne to prison. During the crossing, a storm blew up and the jailers had to release Tell to help row the boat to shore. However, when they reached land, William Tell leapt ashore and pushed the boat back into the lake, where it sank. He then became a leader of the Swiss people in their struggle against the Austrians."

Throughout my career, I knew all these folk tales off by heart (in fact, I still do!) and also knew the exact moment, as we passed a particular house or tree, to start telling the tale, so that we reached the relevant location just as the story reached its climax – in this case, just as we passed the chapel marking the spot where William Tell leapt ashore.

In the far north of Switzerland, close to the German border, the River Rhine, swelled by its passage through Lake Constance, crashes over the most powerful waterfall in Europe. The Rhine Falls are 150m (490ft) wide and 23m (75ft) high – far from being the largest in the world, but the tons of water hurled across each second make it dramatically impressive. As we approached in the coach, we could already hear the roar of the water, and see huge clouds of spray rising, especially in springtime, when the snows were melting in the mountains and the river was at its fullest. When I first visited in the 1980s, it was still possible to drive with the coach down to the riverside so that my less physically able guests could see the Falls without walking far, but (as in so many places in Europe, and the world) increased tourism over the years has demanded increased traffic management – by the 1990s we were obliged to park the coach high on the hillside above the river, leaving guests to walk down the road or else negotiate numerous flights of steps through the trees. Only on one occasion, when I had a guest who used a wheelchair for mobility, did I manage to convince the parking warden to allow us to drive down to the waterside. By the time we reached the Rhine Falls, I had usually managed to 'train' my guests to be punctual (to emphasise the point, I made the last person boarding the coach, if they were late, sing into the microphone!), yet we were often late departing from this visit as guests puffed their way back up the steep slope to the coach park.

In the 1980s I began to learn to ski and after some years I was competent enough to visit some of the more challenging Swiss ski resorts, including Crans Montana (where I broke a small bone in my leg, tripping over an exposed tree root) and Verbier (where I fell from top to bottom of the infamous Tortin black run, surviving unscathed apart from a broken finger) ... but the most memorable was Zermatt in 1991. As it is a traffic-free resort, I arrived by train, disembarking with all my baggage into a swirling snowstorm. The streets were buzzing with sleighs drawn by horses adorned with tinkling bells, and skiers in heavy ski boots were clumping and sliding awkwardly around the bars, chalets and hotels. Zermatt was normally popular with Americans, but in 1991, they had been discouraged from travelling because of tensions in the Middle East and the resort was quite quiet. One day I took the first lift of the day up to the slopes below the massive rocky peak of the Matterhorn, to find myself skiing down a broad slope totally alone, except for a group of Alpine Ibex with massive curving horns, which were trying to flee downhill from me. For some time, I was able to stay with them – till they finally realised that I could move quickly downhill but not uphill, and so changed direction to escape me. A few years later, my company started to offer tours which included two nights in this resort. In the summertime, the horse-drawn sleighs were replaced by electric carts whizzing silently through the streets, but the enchantment was still there. I took my guests on the train up the Gornergrat mountain but left them free to return whenever they wanted – instead offering to escort any who felt fit enough, on a walk down the mountainside through meadows filled with wildflowers, including alpine roses and vivid blue gentians. A magical experience when we were able to escape the usual crowds of tourists, breathing pure mountain air and listening to birdsong as we gradually moved into the forests on the lower slopes of the mountain.

My tours often visited the capital city, Bern, though it is totally unlike the capital city of most countries. It is far from being the largest city in Switzerland (only one third the size of Zurich) and is home to only very few government buildings – the task of governing the country is largely undertaken by the individual 'cantons'. Instead, it is a picturesque town perched high on cliffs above a tight loop of the River Aare. The main street is lined with 4km (2½ mi) of medieval shopping arcades, running between two 14th century gates, one of which houses the Zytglogge – an astronomical clock dating from the 15th century, with moving figures which hourly present a parade of bears and a dancing jester. My guests were always most interested in the Bearpits, where they could see live European Brown Bears, kept in Bern since the 16th century as symbols of the city. When we visited in the 1990s, the bears were still living exclusively in twin stone pits built in the 19th century. Though it was interesting to watch the bears, we could not help but feel the cruelty of keeping wild animals in these confined, stone-lined holes in the ground, with only a small pool of water and a dead tree-trunk to entertain them, watched constantly from above by hordes of visitors. Finally, as the Millennium arrived, the Swiss authorities recognised that they were not keeping the bears properly, and in 2009 they opened a new installation, where green terraces lead down to a large swimming pool beside the river – as I write, a breeding pair of bears and one of their two almost-grown cubs are wandering freely through this much-improved enclosure.

One of the most beautiful regions of Switzerland (in a 'chocolate box' way) is the Bernese Oberland, close by Interlaken: the town itself is not particularly attractive, though it is pleasantly laid out with gardens, but the roads alongside its two lakes are lined with enchanting villages of wooden chalets, their facades adorned with carved panels created centuries ago and re-used in each successive rebuilding. The Swiss are very proud of their homes and most chalets are hung with baskets and window boxes filled with bright red geraniums throughout the summer. One of the most dramatic sights in the region is the gorge of the River Aare, a 2km (just over a mile) stretch of the river running through a ravine sometimes only 1m (3ft) wide. There was never time to fit this attraction into my tours, but I was able to visit when I toured by car in 2005, walking on the hair-raising metal walkway cantilevered out from sheer cliffs (up to 50m/ 160ft high), far above the roaring torrent of the river below. One year, my tour stayed for several nights in the exclusive resort of Grindelwald, a narrow strip of chalets and large hotels squeezed into a deep valley at the foot of the Jungfrau mountain (4158m/ 13600ft). The valley is so tightly confined that it is hard for the sun to penetrate as far as the village except in high summer – on a late season visit, I was glad to escape the chilly gloom of the village streets to walk on the Terassenweg path, deliberately built on the hillside high above the village so that locals and visitors can catch some autumnal sunshine. However, the chance to wake in the morning and watch the first light of dawn illuminating the glistening snowy peaks of the Jungfrau and other surrounding mountains, still made this a special place to stay.

Many of our tours also spent a little time in French-speaking Switzerland, especially in Geneva. I found the city cold and sterile, with ponderous stone mansions housing banks, insurance companies and diplomatic missions. Even its location at the western end of Lake Geneva (locally called Lac Léman), which could be so attractive, is spoiled by the fact that much of the lakeshore is lined with the homes of the wealthy, surrounded by high fences and hedges which block the view of the water to passers-by. The landmark of the city is the Jet d'Eau, a fountain which shoots a spout of water up to 140m (460ft) out of the lake – my guests always wanted to see it, but often it was not functioning as we passed, since it has to be turned off whenever it is windy (otherwise its spray drenches the nearby roads) and it seemed it was always windy in Geneva! Only at the far eastern end of the lake did we find picturesque scenes, where the lakeside villages from Lausanne to Montreux have opened up tree-lined promenades alongside the water, with views across the lake to often snow-capped French alpine peaks. Especially impressive is the 16th century fortress of Chillon, situated just off the shore on a small island, its towers and turrets seeming to rise directly from the water.

Only one area of Switzerland speaks Italian: the 'canton' of Ticino which points southwards into the heart of the Italian Lake District. As we emerged from the Gotthard Tunnel into the province, we immediately felt a different atmosphere all around us. Now on the southern side of the Alps, the weather is often sunnier and warmer, the vegetation more lush and the houses more colourful, with walls painted in soft pinks and yellows. There are pizzerias and sidewalk cafes set out beneath shady trees – it could almost be Italy itself, except that the houses are immaculately maintained and the pavements carefully swept. The people are a strange mixture of Italian panache and Swiss efficiency – a fusion which seems to cause a tension in their character. My tours sometimes called in at the city of Lugano, known as the 'Monte Carlo of Switzerland', with its grand casino, lush gardens and tree-lined lakeside promenade – yet the older part of town is typically Italianate in style, with decorative facades and warm terracotta roofs. Sadly, many of our tours simply rushed through Ticino, heading for the Italian border – I hope one day to return and stay long enough to do it justice!

LIECHTENSTEIN

LIECHTENSTEIN IS THE 4TH SMALLEST COUNTRY in Europe (at 160 km^2/ 62 mi^2, only a little larger than the Welsh capital city of Cardiff). It is an independent principality which is not part of the EU, ruled as a constitutional monarchy by their Prince, yet closely tied to Switzerland – they share a customs union and use the Swiss Franc as their currency. They support no army, relying on the Swiss for defence since 1868: in fact the last action their army saw, was in 1866 when they marched to Austria but arrived too late for the battle. On the way home, they picked up a disgruntled Austrian officer – one of the few occasions in history when an army returned from war with more soldiers than they set out with! Their income comes partly from tourism and partly from financial services – their banks once offered totally secret accounts, but in 2009 they had to reform their banking laws when it became clear that the banks were being used by criminals for money laundering.

Our tours passing from Switzerland to Austria made a stop in the capital, Vaduz, though it offers little of tourist interest, except the opportunity to buy postage stamps in the local post office and to acquire a passport stamp from one of the souvenir shops on the main street … if you make a purchase, of course!

AUSTRIA

AUSTRIA IS NOW A SMALL, relatively unimportant country, yet it is impossible to ignore the fact that it was once one of the greatest powers in Europe (especially if you visit the capital Vienna), at the heart of the Habsburg empire which, in the 16th century, included lands from Italy to Hungary, Spain (including colonies in South America) to the Netherlands ... by the 19th century it had lost the Spanish parts of the empire, but acquired parts of Poland, Bohemia (now Czech Republic), Croatia and the Dalmatian coast. The empire finally collapsed in dramatic fashion after World War 1, when most of its constituent countries gained their independence.

Arriving from Liechtenstein, there is no hint of that glorious history – instead, it was again the mountains which grabbed the attention of my guests. The road plunges beneath the Arlberg Pass in a tunnel opened already in 1978: I never had the opportunity to cross the Pass itself during my tour managing career, though I did ski on the slopes around it one year – a visit notable for periods of heavy snowfall when it was virtually impossible to see even the ground beneath my skis, never mind the views. The tunnel leads into the Austrian state of Tyrol, popular with tourists both summer and winter. I spent a season here in 1976, based in a small village of picturesque painted chalets (though my room was located in a dark, concrete cellar with no view), offering my guests various excursions into the mountains – including a trip along the magnificent Ötztal Valley to the top of the Timmelsjoch Pass (2474m/ 8000ft) where, even in high summer, the road was lined with walls of snow remaining from the previous winter. Our Austrian driver delighted in terrifying the guests as he reversed the rear of the coach right over the abyss, manoeuvring to negotiate tight hairpin bends! Later I made several visits to the Stubai Valley over successive years, learning to ski in the relaxed Austrian way, with much laughter as I fell repeatedly, and restorative sessions afterwards in Neustift's wonderful swimming pool, where it was possible to swim through a plastic curtain out into the open air, floating in deliciously warm water whilst breathing in crisply cold evening air, beneath a sky filled with stars.

Most European tours concentrated only on visiting the capital of Tyrol, Innsbruck, with a small area of historic buildings clustered around the famous Golden Roof (a balcony built by the Habsburg emperor Maximilian in 1500 as a wedding gift to his new bride), though disappointingly the 'golden' tiles are actually just gilded copper. Nearby stands the Hofkirche court church, most notable for Maximilian's massive tomb, surrounded by 24 statues of his illustrious forebears – he claimed to be descended from a range of famous figures who were actually no relation at all, including King Arthur and Mary Queen of Scots! It is an imposing monument, though sadly Maximilian's successor buried him quickly just outside Vienna, and he was never interred in this grand tomb. Innsbruck is proud that it has twice hosted the Winter Olympic games (1964 and 1976) and I always tried to take my guests to see the ski jumps used in both Olympics – an awe-inspiring experience to look up at these soaring towers and to imagine the emotions of the contestants as they stood on the top, looking out over the entire city, but seeing especially the cemetery located almost at the foot of the jump! Alongside the cemetery is Wilten Basilica, a magnificent example of the rococo style of churches found throughout western Austria and south-eastern Germany – its tower topped with an exotic 'onion' dome and its interior filled with stucco decorations painted in white and gold. Whilst in Innsbruck, we attended a Tyrolean-style folklore show – once again with thigh-slapping dances and alpine horns (as in Switzerland), but here performed with less polish and much more genuine pleasure, including ribald comments between the performers (only understandable, of course, for German-speakers). When I first attended these shows, the tour managers and drivers were invited to spend the duration of the performance in a lounge equipped with free whisky and wine – back in the 1980s, it was not unknown for the drivers to sway back to their coaches on rather unsteady legs! Fortunately, stricter traffic regulations and increasing awareness of personal responsibility, meant that the alcoholic drinks were removed by the 1990s and the lounge offered only coffee or tea.

The mountain scenery continued as we moved eastwards towards Salzburg, though I always felt that the landscape was softer and more cultivated here than the wild rocky peaks of Tyrol, perhaps because of the picturesque lakes and villages of the Salzkammergut. Most impressive of all the lakes is the Hallstädtersee, where vertical rocky cliffs rise directly from the water. However, because that lake is difficult to access, we usually stopped instead in Mondsee, a 'chocolate-box pretty' village beside a tranquil lake, where painted houses and sidewalk cafes line the main street. The main attraction is its baroque church, used in the filming of the wedding scenes in the 1965 film 'The Sound of Music' – in fact much of the film was set in locations around the city of Salzburg, so that a whole industry has built up around taking tourists to see those places. On my earlier tours, I was able to stop directly beside a gazebo where my guests could star in their own movies, singing 'I am sixteen, going on seventeen' (or more appropriately 'I am sixty, going on seventy') ... as the years passed, the location became so popular that the authorities had to move the gazebo behind a wall, so my guests could see it but no longer walk inside – tourism is often its own worst enemy!

The city of Salzburg is one of the highlights of any visit to Austria, declared a UNESCO World Heritage site in 1996 – filled with magnificent baroque-style buildings dating from the 17th century when its ruling archbishops were immensely rich because of taxes on the salt from nearby mines, and were determined to make their city the rival of Rome itself. They created vast open piazzas with central fountains surrounded by grand palaces, and built 27 ornate churches – the finest of all being the cathedral, a vast expanse of marble pillars and arches, adorned with plaster decorations and paintings. The archbishops also prided themselves on their sponsorship of artists and musicians, including Mozart in his youth. He was born in Salzburg in 1756, in a house which still sits in the heart of the old town, on the main street (Getreidegasse) – now a pedestrianised tourist hotspot, famous for the elaborate wrought iron signs which act as advertising boards for the various shops and businesses lining the street.

Though my guests always enjoyed their visits to Salzburg, the city was partly spoiled for me by the numbers of tourists there and the complication of trying to ensure that my group was able to do and see what they wanted, despite those crowds. It is always difficult when one destination becomes world-famous, so that everyone visiting the country is determined to see it – though there were other equally interesting and beautiful places I could have shown them instead. I particularly love Graz (though it is not on most tourist routes), in the south-eastern province of Steiermark, which is also a UNESCO World Heritage site with a magnificently preserved old town, filled with grand palaces erected over the course of many centuries, some with facades decorated with colourful murals. The centre is totally pedestrianised, which caused some difficulties for us since our hotel was located on one of those traffic-free streets – we were asked not to arrive too early, so that the businesses along the street would be closed and there would not be too many pedestrians to avoid as our coach crept slowly towards the hotel door.

In the far east of Austria lies Vienna, capital of today's country and at one time the capital of the entire vast Habsburg empire. My guests were always excited to visit the city, though to me its atmosphere seemed to lack vivacity, with Viennese citizens nostalgic for their imperial past rather than looking forward to a modern future. There is still an active 'coffee culture' in the city, with innumerable cafes scattered throughout both city centre and suburbs, where customers can order a single coffee (and perhaps a slice of tempting cake) and then sit for hours reading the newspapers or chatting – the coffee is served on a silvered tray with a glass of cold water, which is changed once an hour throughout the customer's stay. Also typical of this obsession with tradition, is the almost 200-year-old dispute (still ongoing) between two pastry shops as to which actually created the world-famous chocolate Sacher Torte. Vienna's streets are lined with the huge city-palaces of European noble families, some still belonging to descendants of those same families – in the winter season, many Viennese attend a series of formal balls held in these palaces, enjoying the opportunity to dress up in imperial style and dream of their glorious history.

Sightseeing in the city took us around the Ringstrasse, a broad avenue built in the 19th century on the site of the demolished city walls, lined with imposing buildings in a range of architectural styles – from the heavy, classical stonework of the Opera House and State Theatre, to the multitude of spires adorning the neo-Gothic City Hall and the wide Greek-style facade of the Parliament: all beautifully illuminated by night. A highlight for my guests was a tour of Schönbrunn Palace, summer palace of the Habsburg emperors, filled with magnificent artworks and furnishings. We always used a specialist guide for these tours, leaving me free to complete paperwork or occasionally to escort guests to embassies to amend incorrect visas or acquire temporary travel papers if they had lost their passports – however, I cannot forget the occasion when our specialist guide did not arrive at our meeting place, and I was obliged to conduct the tour myself. I had quite a store of miscellaneous titbits about Habsburg history and 18th century architecture, but nowhere near the quantity of information being presented to the groups ahead of and behind us – how embarrassing to have to stand silently with my guests, waiting for another guide to finish their detailed commentary so that we could progress to the next room.

Amazingly, in the late 1980s Vienna's deeply traditional cityscape suddenly began to be transformed by examples of modernistic architecture from a 20th century Viennese artist called Hundertwasser. I had never heard of him, but was fascinated to spot, as we drove from one side of the city to the other, the multi-coloured facade and sparkling mirrored chimney now clothing a waste treatment plant. Our city guide seemed unimpressed and reluctant to give me any information about it, but further research led me to a housing block built by the same architect (opened in 1986). It was difficult to access by coach, since it was located in a district of narrow streets, but I eventually managed to add it to my regular sightseeing route – an astounding building which blended architecture and nature, with undulating floors, grass-covered roof and trees growing out from the windows. I later saw another of his creations in the eastern German city of Magdeburg, the last building Hundertwasser designed before his death in 2000 (though it was only built 2004-05). In my opinion, these constructions rival those of the much more famous Spanish architect Gaudí – but will they become equally important tourist sights?

When I first began to bring guests to Vienna in the late 1970s, my groups were able to visit the stables of the Spanish Riding School, to see the famous Lipizzaner horses in their stalls (though tickets for actual performances were too expensive and too difficult to obtain at such short notice). On one occasion, I was even able to take a special group to visit the stud farm at Piber, in south eastern Austria – an interesting experience for me, since the breeder who escorted us spoke no English, so I had to translate his explanations ... though I did not know any of the specialist horse-breeding terms he was using. I later learned that Vollblut ('full-blood') actually translates as 'thoroughbred', and the action of a stallion on a mare is called 'covering'. As I interpreted, I had to dilute some of the vitriolic comments which the breeder made when he learned that my guests were mainly Australians – he claimed that Australia had been sold a couple of stallions in 1975, for performance purposes only, but had begun to breed from them, thus breaking the carefully monitored bloodlines of the official Austrian studbook (I later watched a performance of these magnificent animals whilst visiting Sydney, and was very impressed!). Sadly, these visits were stopped abruptly in 1983, when an outbreak of a new form of Equine Herpes devastated the stud farm and it was realised that there was a huge infection risk in allowing casual visitors close to the animals. However, I had learned enough to be able to tell future groups about the Lipizzaner horses – born dark brown and usually turning white between the ages of 6-10 years old; stallions brought to Vienna to begin training at the age of 4; young horses taught by experienced riders (and vice-versa) for 6 years; then only the most talented stallions taught the dramatic 'airs above the ground' (the movements which feature on every postcard). The mares remain at the stud farm, given only minimal training to assess any potential natural skills which they could pass on to their foals.

Many of the greatest Germanic musicians were drawn to Vienna during its Golden Age and my guests often asked if I could arrange a concert for them. In the 1970s and 80s, all I could offer was a poor-quality performance in the grounds of the Kursalon pavilion, so I was pleased when suddenly several entrepreneurs recognised the opportunity and began to offer concerts in the magnificent city palaces. What a delight for my passengers to sweep up the grand double staircase to the ornate ballroom of Palais Auersperg, sitting beneath glittering chandeliers as a chamber orchestra played airs by Mozart and Strauss. In total contrast were evenings spent in one of the wine villages set amid vineyards in the hills surrounding the city, where we enjoyed a dinner of chunky meats, especially chicken and succulent pork, with salads and apple strudel, entertained throughout by musicians playing popular songs as they wandered among the tables. All the time my guests were drinking mugfuls of the Heurige wine (only made the previous year and still sharp and immature) – it slipped down easily … then kicked like a mule! Often I had to support or steer guests back to the coach at the end of the evening, protesting that they wanted to stay longer – though I knew that we had an early start next day. To prolong the evening's fun, I tried to keep the entire group singing all the way back to the hotel (up to an hour's drive, depending on which wine village we visited). Though I am not really an extrovert, my professional image as a tour manager had me dancing down the aisle of the coach, swinging an umbrella as we sang 'Singing in the rain', and we often managed a hilarious version of 'There's a hole in my bucket', with one side of the coach singing in a deep masculine voice and the other side singing a high falsetto for the female part – I had to sing both, to keep everyone going.

In the forested hills to the south of Vienna lies the little town of Mayerling, where the Habsburg emperors kept a small hunting lodge – location of one of history's most romantic tragedies. The emperor ruling at the time was Franz Josef, a stern and autocratic leader, trying desperately to hold together an empire which, just a few years later, would be torn apart by WW1. His only son and heir was Crown Prince Rudolf, a sensitive and poetic young man who did not get on well with his father. In 1889, trapped in a loveless, political marriage, he fell in love with a beautiful teenage baroness, Maria – however, when he asked his father for permission to divorce his wife and marry his mistress, Franz Josef was outraged and refused point-blank to consider the idea. So Rudolf and Maria took their carriage off for one last night in Mayerling before completing a suicide pact – Rudolf shot Maria, sitting by her body for several hours before shooting himself. Franz Josef was devastated and tried to hush up the scandal by having Maria's body smuggled out of the hunting lodge secretly, then issuing a statement saying that Rudolf had died of a heart attack. The true story did not take long to emerge, however, and Rudolf's final death certificate stated that he died 'while the balance of his mind was disturbed'. The new heir to the throne was Franz Josef's nephew, Franz Ferdinand – whose assassination sparked WW1 and the collapse of the entire Habsburg empire.

Italy - Naples

THE ITALIAN PENINSULA

ITALY

WHAT A CONTRAST WHEN WE travelled from the well-ordered lifestyle of Switzerland or Austria, into the colourful and passionate chaos of Italy! As we entered the country, I had to deliver instructions on 'how to survive Italy' to my (mostly Australian and New Zealander) guests – they expected polite queues instead of the forceful, multi-headed 'knot' favoured by Italians when waiting at a cash-till or museum entrance; they were accustomed to sending the husband to harangue hotel receptionists if there was a fault in their rooms, when most Italians respond far more willingly to a coy smile and eyelash-fluttering feminine request for help. I also had to try to explain that there is no such thing as 'typical Italian' food or crafts – there are huge variations in architecture, culture and even language from one region to the next, and even larger differences between the relatively rich north of the country and the often poverty-stricken south. The country of Italy has only existed since unification in 1861, after centuries when different parts of the Italian peninsula formed completely independent states, often at war with each other – so my guests should not expect to eat pizza in Venice (it is typical of Naples), nor to buy leather goods in Rome (when it is a Florentine craft).

Most distinctive of all the Italian cities is Venice, built on a cluster of islands in the middle of a tidal lagoon – the tides are now partially controlled by electronic gates, but when I visited with a friend in October 2015, we managed to arrive as high water (Aqua Alta) flooded the streets, so we had to remove our shoes and wade to our hotel barefoot! There is no vehicular access beyond the end of the bridge carrying road and railway from the mainland – to get around the city, there are 'vaporetto' water-buses on the main canals, romantic gondolas (now used mainly as an expensive tourist experience) on the side canals ... or simply your own two feet. Travelling by boat along the Grand Canal past the magnificent (if now rather run-down) palaces of rich merchants, or visiting St Mark's Basilica with its marble decorations, golden mosaics and jewel-encrusted altars, it is easy to remember that this city was once one of the richest and most powerful nations in the world. My first sight of the city was in 1978, travelling by train from Florence (where I was learning Italian) for a brief weekend visit. We stayed in a 'cheap and cheerful' guesthouse (money was tight in those days) with paper peeling off the damp walls, and shutters difficult to open because the building was no longer straight. But what a thrill to experience this unique city for the first time, fighting past crowds of hotel porters touting for trade in the station lobby, to emerge beside the Grand Canal ... I had not realised that there are absolutely no cars in Venice, nor even roads to put them on – just canals and narrow, twisting alleys to be followed on foot, doubling back and forth as I sought the next bridge.

On my earliest professional tours to the city, I had to advise my guests to remain in the immediate environs of St Mark's Square so that they did not get lost and miss their shuttle-boat back to the budget hotels we were using on the mainland. However, when I started working with a higher-quality tour company, our accommodation changed to hotels in the heart of island Venice – now I could recommend to my guests that they allow themselves to get lost in the tortuous, winding alleyways, following occasional arrows painted on the walls, pointing towards the railway station or Rialto Bridge. Without the stress of possibly missing a transfer, this is by far the best way to explore the city – ducking under archways, scrambling over high-arched bridges, peering through rotting water-gates into the docks of historic palaces ... and if you are still exploring as darkness falls, watching as magnificent glass chandeliers are illuminated in the grand salons of the upper storeys.

I was often able to offer my guests an excursion by boat out into the lagoon to visit some of the other islands. We called at a peaceful Franciscan monastery (San Francesco del Deserto), escorted through the island's tree-filled gardens and tranquil cloisters by a delightfully characterful monk, then moved on to the fishing community of Burano. This island is higher than most parts of Venice, so does not flood at high tide – the small houses are free of mould and damp, and brilliantly painted in a multitude of different colours. Here we strolled through narrow paved passages, often hearing the sweet song of caged canaries hung outside the windows, past doorways where women were busily working in the sunshine on intricate pieces of lace for sale in the local shops. The highlight of our visit was a delicious lunch, a continuous stream of locally caught fishes of many types, simply cooked and served with salads – many of my guests were only used to eating seafood in the form of steaks cut from huge ocean fish, so I had to conduct a brief lesson in how to fillet the tiny St Peter's fish (like a very small plaice), before they plunged wildly into their food and filled their mouths with bones!

Verona is another of my favourite Italian cities – our itineraries usually included a brief stop to admire the so-called 'Juliet's Balcony', overlooking the courtyard of a house once belonging to the Cappello family (supposedly the inspiration for Shakespeare's Capulets). The balcony itself was of limited interest, beyond the opportunity for a photo with the bronze statue of Juliet outside – perhaps clasping her (now highly polished) breast! However, in order to reach the balcony, we had to walk past a magnificent 1st century Arena, one of the most complete Roman structures in the world and still used for opera performances, and then make our way through atmospheric pedestrianised streets full of elegant Italian fashion stores and tempting ice-cream shops. I loved the warm, friendly atmosphere of these narrow lanes – a wonderful introduction to the best of Italian life.

Speeding along the Italian motorways, flying via bridges and tunnels through the Apennine Mountains which form the 'backbone' of the Italian peninsula, it is only a relatively short drive to Florence – a medieval city of cobbled streets and Renaissance palaces, with austere churches enlivened by elaborate marble facades. I came to know the city quite well when I spent two months learning Italian there during the winter of 1978, describing my first impressions in a letter to my parents:

"Florence is not famous so much for just one or two buildings, but rather for the city as a whole. It still seems to live in the Middle Ages, when the wealthy Medici brought the Renaissance to the city. The streets are narrow and lined with what were once palaces – though it is now hazardous to walk down these narrow streets, dodging the cars in the road and the dog-dirt on the pavements! The Florentine people still gather on street corners to chat and, between 6-7.30pm, the streets are full of shoppers since the shops stay open into the early evening. There are hundreds of small restaurants and trattorie in all parts of the city, where you can eat well for a reasonable price – and they are almost always full of friendly Florentines, ready to offer advice on what to choose from the menu."

We ate regularly at a family-run trattoria near our accommodation, popping our heads into the kitchen before taking a seat, to choose whichever dish looked and smelled best. We came to know most of the regular guests, chatting easily with them in our gradually improving Italian – though I will not forget the occasion when I was interrupted while talking to several male customers, by the arrival of an (off-duty) policeman I had got to know – he whipped out his gun when he saw me talking to other men! Fortunately, I managed to defuse his angry jealousy and sent him packing, telling him to walk the streets until I had finished my meal and was ready to meet up with him. Needless to say, this story did not feature in my letters to my parents!

Sadly, my first enchantment with the city was later spoiled by the stresses of trying to make it a pleasant visit for my guests, especially as tourism has developed over the years and Florence has become more and more crowded with visitors. The narrow medieval streets mean that there is no access for coaches, so all sightseeing has to be on foot – pleasurable when you are young and fit, but difficult for many of my more elderly passengers, especially when they were forced to remain strictly with the group for the entire duration of the 2-3 hour walking tour (so they did not get lost) despite their varied interests: some were fascinated to hear the guide's stories from the city's glorious past, but many were focused only on shopping for fine Florentine leatherwork and gold, while others were desperate to see as many Renaissance art treasures as possible. I came to dread our visits to Florence, though one abiding delight remained the sculptures of Michelangelo – especially in the Academia

Museum. Here I usually ignored the milling hordes around his statue of David and instead admired the half-finished sculptures of the Slaves, only the front of their bodies emerging (in full detail) from the rough stone, as if they are fighting their way out of the block and just need to be freed by the artist's chisel.

Almost every weekend of that stay in Florence in 1978, was spent visiting other destinations in northern Italy – some of which became part of the regular routine once I began to escort tours to Italy, though others remained just a distant memory. Of course, I made the short journey to Pisa to see the famous Leaning Tower – climbing to the top was a weird sensation, akin to sea-sickness, as my eyes told my brain that I was climbing upwards whilst my legs were telling me that the steps were sloping downwards! My language school also organised a trip out into the Tuscan hills, winding our way up a twisting road to the tiny walled town of San Gimignano, still bristling with towers which its inhabitants built to defend themselves from attack. We arrived in the middle of the pre-Lent Carnival, with three huge floats being toured through the town to the accompaniment of music from two rival bands, while small children in fancy-dress threw confetti all over everyone, and older children ran through the streets hitting anyone they could with (very hard) plastic truncheons. Nearby we visited Siena with its ornate cathedral – the facade was overpowering enough, with its carvings and embellishments ... but to find the interior striped in black and white marble like a zebra, with elaborate altars, inlaid marble floors and even busts representing the heads of all the Popes around the main aisle, was too much for me! It was in this cathedral that I first realised that Italy is able to use as much marble as it likes, since the country has such large supplies of the stone – it is not an expensive luxury, like at home. However, I love Siena's central square (where they run the bloodthirsty Palio horse race twice a year) – narrow, convoluted, sunless streets lead to an oval Piazza which is usually full of both sunshine and Sienese people, sipping cappuccino or wine at open-air cafes.

Heading southwards, some of my tours made a detour into the foothills of the Apennines to visit the hilltop town of Assisi – famous as the home of St Francis (patron saint of animals and the environment), but notable to me for its delightful stone-built architecture and splendid views over the valley below. In the valley stands the massive basilica of Santa Maria degli Angeli – a huge baroque church built around a tiny stone chapel supposedly erected by St Francis himself and now covered in fresco paintings. St Francis, with his very simple lifestyle, is credited with introducing the crib to our Christmas festivities (as a reminder of the simplicity of Christ's birth) – when I visited the basilica in the month of December, I found it filled with nativity scenes in every size and degree of detail. Assisi is also associated with one of my most difficult tour managing memories: as we drove along the motorways towards the town, one of my guests suffered a heart attack in the coach and died before we could fetch help. I left the group to continue to our hotel with the driver, whilst I escorted his body and his family to the nearest hospital, putting the family into contact with the appropriate consular team, before I made my way by public transport to Assisi to rejoin the group. I had to inform them that their fellow guest had been confirmed dead on arrival at hospital (one of the first instructions drummed into me during the brief training course I had undertaken before starting my career, was never to allow a guest to be declared dead inside the coach, since that meant the coach would be impounded). Obviously, the news cast a pall over our tour, which I felt I had to dispel so that the remainder of the group could continue to enjoy their holiday. I bought some black-edged writing paper and asked my guests to write messages to the dead man's family, which I forwarded to their home – fortunately, this seemed to ease the group's sadness, and we continued with an otherwise very successful tour.

Every time my tours visited Italy, of course we visited Rome. My first sight of Italy's capital was again in 1978, when I spent the final week of my Italian sojourn in the city, sharing a cheap hotel room with the girlfriend with whom I had been studying Italian, but also exploring with the Sicilian policeman who had befriended me in Florence and who knew Rome well. He marched me for hours through the streets on my first day in the city, finishing up sitting beside the illuminated Trevi Fountain munching on goat-cheese sandwiches and watching the hordes of tourists tossing coins over their left (or was it their right?) shoulders – a good introduction to the romance of Rome. On that first visit, I had time to descend into the site of the Roman Forum, absorbing the history as I walked on ancient stone roads from temple to temple; to stroll among the ruined palaces on the Palatine Hill; to explore the vast Baths of Caracalla; even to spend a day wandering along the remnants of the Appian Way, stopping to visit the Catacombs of St Sebastian (where I was guided with extreme haste by a student whose English was incomprehensible) and of St Callistus (where I was guided by a monk who explained everything very patiently). It was a sobering thought to imagine the persecution which drove Christians into these damp, dark tunnels with only tiny lights … yet I could also imagine the Spirit-filled rejoicing of those who had worshipped there.

This is how ancient Rome should be enjoyed, with time to explore at leisure and to stop and visualise what life was like in ancient times. Unfortunately, as a tour manager, it was not the way I could introduce my guests to the glories of Rome. We usually had just one day to show them everything they wanted to see, starting with the treasures of the Vatican – the immense basilica of St Peter's and the Vatican Museums, where we were hustled past galleries filled with magnificent paintings and precious artifacts to reach the Sistine Chapel, a masterpiece rendered almost invisible by the packed crowds of visitors. Our explorations of ancient Rome were limited to a viewpoint over the Forum from which the guide could point out the various ruined buildings, and a glimpse inside the Colosseum (again pushing and shoving to get to a spot from which my guests could get a clear view across the remains of the animal pens and prisons once hidden beneath a long-vanished floor). When I first escorted tours to Rome, I was at least able to offer my passengers a peaceful evening drive around the heart of the city, stopping frequently to allow them a good view of various landmarks whilst there was little traffic to obstruct us, to climb the Capitoline Hill for a spectacular view over the illuminated Forum and to stop in the enchanting Piazza Navona to sample a 'tartufo' ice cream. However, as the years passed and tourism grew ever more intense, the police had to respond by positioning themselves at every sightseeing highlight, blowing whistles and gesturing frantically to 'move on' (with the threat of fines if we did not obey). In my last years as a tour manager, when fortunately I no longer conducted tours into Italy, colleagues told me that it was now impossible to travel by coach into the city – instead our poor guests, whatever their age or mobility, had to either pack themselves into public buses or else walk right across the heart of Rome. I doubt any of them could have returned home with magical memories of the city they had travelled so far to see.

The only taste of southern Italy which most of my guests received, was as we hurtled on the motorways past the port of Naples towards the ruins of the ancient Roman city of Pompeii, buried for centuries by the eruption of Mount Vesuvius in 79 AD. However, the Neapolitan people's desperate scrabble to make a living was immediately evident as soon as we drew up at the entrance to the archaeological site – the roads were lined with men in peaked caps, gesturing in an authoritative manner towards one of the multiple parking areas, each trying to convince wavering motorists that this was the official place where they should stop. Alongside the parking wardens were people waving multipacks of cigarettes, armfuls of bamboo seat-covers, handfuls of cigarette lighters (or whatever else had recently been illegally smuggled out of the port) for sale through the car windows ... or children carrying a bucket of soapy water and a squeegee, ready to give your windscreen a slapdash clean. Several of my drivers told tales of stopping at traffic lights in the city of Naples itself, to find that their rear lights were swiftly removed – only to be offered to them for sale at the next traffic light! As my guests disembarked from the coach, they were inundated by insistent vendors of postcards, sunhats or souvenir fragments of 'ancient pottery' – my first priority was to carve a passage through the melee for my group to reach the gates, so they could pass through into the relative tranquility of Pompeii's ruined streets. In its defence, when I stayed in Naples in 2017, I found a city transformed by a new, energetic mayor – the streets were mostly clean, a new metro system had reduced the chaotic traffic and I wandered freely without any threat of tricksters, muggings or pickpockets. What a joy to see that things can improve over the years, as well as worsen!

In Pompeii, the challenge was the usual problem of trying to keep the group together and within earshot of their guide, as innumerable other groups were herded around us. In recent years, I have often seen local guides with a discreet microphone linked to individual headsets worn by each member of their group: a fantastic technological development, reducing the hubbub caused by the shouted commentaries of multiple guides clustered around a single 'sight'. Despite all the hassle, however, Pompeii is a venue which should not be missed – an evocative chance to walk on original Roman streets, where carts and chariots have worn ruts into the stones, past drinking booths with counters still pierced by the holes which supported amphorae of wine, and houses still adorned with frescoed walls. In 1980, Queen Elizabeth and Prince Philip visited Pompeii: one of the local guides told me that the authorities wished to spare her the sight of some of the more erotic images frescoed on the walls of the villas and so positioned site wardens in front of them as the royal party passed by ... Prince Philip's curiosity was aroused, so he asked the wardens to move out of the way and carefully inspected the images for himself.

Highlight for many of my guests were cement representations of some of Pompeii's residents, buried in solidified ash before their bodies were vaporised, leaving a hole which could be used as a mould to create figures detailed enough to show even the expressions on their faces as they died. When I revisited the area in 2017, I had the chance to visit Herculaneum, a much smaller town also destroyed by Vesuvius in 79 AD, but this time swallowed up by mud and lava which even preserved some of the wooden roofs and balconies on the homes. In the early years when I passed the site, I used to tell my guests that the excavations here had revealed no bodies, so it was assumed that the residents had escaped. However in the 1980s, excavations reached the buildings which once stood along the seashore – they found ancient boatsheds piled high with bones, the remains of people who died clutched together and gasping for air. The bodies in Pompeii were vaporised in extreme heat, but this new evidence showed that the people of Herculaneum died suffocated by mud, trapped on the edge of the sea without boats to escape.

From Pompeii our tours generally continued around the Bay of Naples on twisting roads beneath soaring cliffs to the pleasant resort of Sorrento (the roads on the opposite side of the peninsula are even more precipitous – the 'Amalfi Drive' is forbidden to full-size coaches for safety reasons). From Sorrento we took a day trip across to the enchanting Isle of Capri. The initial impressions were again of crowds, but I found that most tourists arrived at the port and immediately packed themselves either into the funicular railway or into minibuses to travel up to the Piazzetta in Capri Town, where they stayed. If you walked for just a few minutes deeper into the village, it was easy to escape the other visitors – and when I was lucky enough to escort tours which actually stayed in hotels on the island for a night, I discovered that most visitors returned home at the end of the day, leaving the village in idyllic peace. We used specially-built tiny buses which roared at hair-raising speed along narrow roads between the vines and orange groves, past the community of Anacapri on the highest part of the island and on to the cliffs above the famous Blue Grotto. A long flight of steps took us down to the sea, where our guides waved and shouted frantically to entice several of the rowing boats bobbing on the ocean to pull over to us, loading my guests precariously as the waves surged around them, then hovering at the entrance to the cave until a wave retreated far enough to leave space for them to shoot inside. What a magical scene awaited them! Most of this sea-cave's entrance is below water, so the sun's rays are filtered by the impossibly blue sea water through which they pass, bathing the entire huge cavern in blue light. The visit was a logistical nightmare for me and the guides … we never knew how long it would take to get the whole group into boats, but it was worth the wait!

Some of my European tours travelled further south to the ports of Bari or Brindisi, to embark on ferries to Greece, and I was fascinated to glimpse in the fields strange conical huts called 'trulli'. To learn more, in 2017 I joined a tour of Puglia (the region covering the 'heel' of Italy's 'boot') which took me into the heart of 'trulli' country at the village of Alberobello. We arrived in a pleasant village square lined with pavement cafes (and thick with sweating tourists – the temperature was 34°C), with semi-pedestrianised, marble-paved roads leading uphill through a forest of conical, grey stone roofs, as if the hillside had erupted in an outbreak of pustules. I was delighted to discover that our hotel was composed of clusters of these individual 'trulli' homes, each forming a single hotel room. Passing through my own front door I found a small lounge beneath a high conical ceiling, which sucked the hot air upwards to cool the room; to one side was a small, vaulted alcove just big enough for my bed and another alcove housed a compact bathroom – exactly the characterful hotel I had hoped for.

Our tour moved on to Taranto, at first sight a thriving industrial city and naval port – in 1970 a huge steelworks (largest in Europe) was built outside the city and the population abandoned their city centre homes and moved nearer to the source of wealth. However, in 2012 the steelworks was closed by the Italian government for blatantly ignoring pollution controls – a huge proportion of the population was thrown out of work and serious corruption absorbed what little money was left in the city. A long history of wealth and influence (the city's National Archaeological Museum contains a treasury of gold jewellery and mosaics from Taranto's 1st Golden Age in the 4th century AD, while their 2nd Golden Age in the 18th and 19th centuries has left innumerable magnificent palaces) was tragically lost to 21st century mismanagement and corruption. I was so saddened to see the condition of the old town – the waterfront lined with boarded-up buildings blackened by mould, though washing hanging outside, indicated that some buildings were still inhabited; once glorious palaces with fine facades and ornate window-frames, mostly now crumbling away with windows and doors sealed up with breeze blocks. With some investment, this could be a glorious baroque city to rival nearby Lecce, but it seems that no-one has money for Taranto.

Crossing into the region of Basilicata, we came to another amazing destination: Matera. Its streets of baroque mansions and ornate church facades were pleasant, but seemed nothing special till suddenly a gap between the buildings gave me a first glimpse of the 'Sassi' – a vast quarry-like hole in the hillside, filled with vaulted buildings clinging to the cliffs: Matera's 'city of caves'. Over the centuries, the poorest citizens had been forced down the sides of the ravine, enlarging natural caves with rooms stuck to the side of the cliffs like swallows' nests; meanwhile the richest citizens were building their palaces on the clifftop, where the main town still stands. Gradually the 'cave city' grew in population until it could no longer provide adequate water and sanitation – by 1952 there were 20,000 people living in appalling conditions there. On a visit to the town, the Italian President declared the Sassi a 'national shame' and ordered that the population be forcibly evicted and re-housed in hastily erected apartment blocks. Over the next 30 years, the cave-city became a dangerous district, infamous for drug-dealing and illegal sexual activities. Then in the 1980s a few artists rediscovered its charms and the government started offering grants to restore the cave homes. In 1993 the United Nations gave the town World Heritage status and tourists started to visit, so some of the caves were transformed into unique hotels – we stayed in one, sleeping beneath rock ceilings and breakfasting from a rock-cut buffet. What a unique city!

As a tour manager, I often travelled out of Italy to France via the dramatic motorway which cuts through the Apennine Mountains as they fall into the sea east of Genoa, a continuous series of dark tunnels (over 130 within a

160km/ 100mi stretch of road), interspersed with short bridges offering views over sunlit valleys and sparkling blue sea. As we passed by, I would tell my guests about a region called the Cinque Terre (though I had never seen it) – a landslide-prone, mountainous landscape of terraced vineyards and olive groves, with colourful villages clinging to the cliffs beside the sea. It was originally accessible only on foot or by boat, until in 1874 a railway was built to link the villages – an engineering marvel which required 23 bridges and 51 tunnels to travel just 44km (27mi). In the 20th century a few precarious and difficult mountain roads were built to give access to the villages from the land, so, at the end of the summer season in 1994, I decided to rent a car and finally visit the Cinque Terre. Despite the fact that I was plagued by heavy rain which brought the hillsides sliding down across the roads, I was enchanted by the colourful villages – each a jumble of houses, squeezed into a narrow ravine opening on to the sea, sometimes with fishing boats pulled up to block the end of the single narrow village street. I picked my way cautiously down to several of these communities, and then spent a few hours following one of the original walking trails to the tiny waterside monastery of San Fruttuoso, still accessible only by foot or boat. Definitely somewhere to visit again!

SAN MARINO

THIS IS THE WORLD'S OLDEST republic, reputedly founded in 301 AD by St Marinus and achieving its current size in 1463. It has managed to maintain its independence over the centuries, mainly because it is perched on an inaccessible rock which is hard to conquer, and still enacts its own laws and issues its own stamps. However, it is closely tied to Italy (the country which totally encloses it), uses Italian as its official language and the Euro as its currency (though it is not part of the EU). It is the 3rd smallest country in Europe (62km²/ 24mi²), with a tiny population of just 34,000.

I visited San Marino during my Italian sojourn in the winter of 1978, intending to stay one night, travelling by rail from Florence to Rimini then by bus up to San Marino. The higher the bus climbed, the more snow appeared – when I finally reached the town clinging to the top of its rock, I found it thick with snow and with iced-over paths. The whole place seemed deserted – no tourists, no locals. I went first to the cathedral where I was spotted by an obviously tourist-trained verger, who took me for a flying tour of the church (including hopping in and out of the twin beds of St Marino and St Leo, carved out of the rock) and then sold me a guidebook. I continued to the town hall where an equally adept porter gave me a potted history of San Marino and tried to sell me some special-issue stamps. After slithering precariously along the path between two of the fortresses, I decided it was pointless to stay overnight, and returned to my base in Florence.

VATICAN CITY

THOUGH, AS TOURISTS, WE PASSED easily in and out of the Vatican during our visits to Rome, in fact the Vatican City is an independent city state, administered by the Holy See with the Pope as its sovereign. It has an area of just 0.5km² (0.2mi²) and a population of approximately 825 – making it the smallest independent state in the world, both in terms of area and population. Citizenship is available only to those working for the Holy See, and their families, but cannot be inherited – if someone no longer qualifies, they can instead claim Italian citizenship. There is a small Vatican police force, but no army – the famous Swiss Guards are employed only as personal bodyguards for the Pope. This group of approximately 130 soldiers are still recruited directly from Switzerland, as they have been since the 16th century – required to be Catholic, unmarried, aged 19-30, and to have completed their basic training in the Swiss military. Though they look so picturesque in their medieval-style uniforms (according to legend, originally designed by Michelangelo), they are actually highly trained both in weaponry and bodyguarding techniques – those traditional battleaxes are supplemented by hidden guns!

The state is basically composed only of St Peter's Square and Basilica, the Vatican Museums, papal palaces and gardens ... though it also includes several of the major basilica churches in Rome and the papal summer palace in Castel Gondolfo, in the hills south of Rome. My guests rarely appreciated that they were passing from one state to another as they scuttled through the hectic Italian traffic of Via Della Conciliazione into the relative safety of St Peter's Square, nor that they were leaving Italy behind as they finally reached the head of an impossibly long queue for the Vatican Museums and started the long climb up the ramps leading to the galleries … but in fact, they were ticking off one more country from their bucket lists. For me, as a tour manager, visiting the Vatican meant one more opportunity for my guests to lose themselves in the milling crowds – especially when their local guide planned to take them through the hidden passage from the Sistine Chapel directly into St Peter's Basilica (a route forbidden to individual tourists without a qualified local guide): I was told by several distressed guests, "the group just disappeared". After several bad experiences, I ensured that everyone had their hotel list with them before setting off for the day's sightseeing … at least then, they could show it to a taxi driver and find their way home, hopefully before we departed the city next day.

Spain - Santiago

THE IBERIAN PENINSULA

SPAIN

THE IBERIAN PENINSULA (OF WHICH 79% is occupied by Spain) seems to sit at the extremity of Europe, attached to the rest of the continent only by a 650km (400 mi) border with France. It is not a country which a tourist would pass through, en route to somewhere else, and consequently many European tours do not visit it. Yet the region was ruled for 600 years by the Romans, who built some amazing structures which we can still see today ... then by the Germanic Visigoth tribes (who left little for tourists to see) ... then in the 8th century it was occupied by Muslim Moors (coming from North Africa), who left a tremendous legacy of culture and architecture. They ruled for 700 years and made their realm of Al-Andalus into a major economic and intellectual centre. Gradually several Christian kingdoms developed in the north and eventually pushed the Moors out of Iberia, the last leaving in 1492. For 300 years, Spain then developed one of the largest empires in history (including parts of Italy and the Netherlands, Texas, Mexico and most of South America) – Spanish is still the 2nd most spoken native language in the world (after Chinese), and the country is full of ornate churches decorated with gold brought home by treasure fleets from the Americas. Through the 19th century the empire crumbled, and in 1931 the king was sent into exile. Spain became a Republic – but almost immediately it was plunged into a vicious civil war between royalists and Franco's fascists, which saw half a million Spaniards killed and another half million fleeing into exile. Franco won the war and ruled with a firm authoritarian hand until his death in 1975 – when I first visited the country in the late 1970s, heavily armed police were still a common sight on street corners. When Franco died, the king was invited to return – still ruling as a constitutional monarch today.

Although Spain has been ruled by a single government for hundreds of years, some regions (notably Catalonia and the Basque lands) have preserved a strong sense of their separate identity – so my European tours which travelled only as far as Barcelona (capital of Catalonia), found a completely different atmosphere from the rest of Spain (and even a different language, often closer to French than to Castilian Spanish). I love this lively city, especially the Ramblas street – an elegant tree-lined avenue, filled with booths selling flowers and postcards, where street musicians play and 'living statues' pose in the central promenade, though heavy traffic fills the outer lanes. My tours often stayed in a hotel on the Ramblas, where we desperately hoped that the staff had reserved a spot near the door for us to unload baggage – sometimes unhelpful cars nibbled away at the space so that we could not park, and then had to block all the (very impatient) traffic while we unloaded passengers and their suitcases. Although Barcelona is a relaxed and vibrant place, it also has major problems with casual crime from pickpockets and opportunistic thieves – I always posted a couple of passengers beside our pile of luggage as it was unloaded on to the pavement, to guard it until the porters could carry it inside (it was not unknown for someone to pick up a suitcase and scurry away with it, if no-one was looking). On one unforgettable occasion, my tour was booked into an alternative hotel in a side street off the Ramblas – but no-one had warned us not to drive in to the hotel's front door. Once in, the driver could not get out – it was too narrow to drive forwards, and was officially a one-way street, so he could not reverse out. It took a lot of effort to release him!

Official sightseeing took us into the narrow pedestrianised streets of the old town, as far as the original cathedral. The church itself is a typical Gothic structure from the 14th century, with ornate golden altars looming from dark niches surrounding the main aisle. What an unexpected treat it was, when we emerged from this gloomy interior into the cloisters behind the church, with a shady garden and a pond filled with noisy white geese. Also popular with my guests was Catalonia Square with its fountains, illuminated and 'dancing' to music in the evenings ... and behind the square, the Spanish Village where typical buildings from different regions of Spain have been erected side-by-side, dotted with restaurants and shops selling regional specialities, to give a flavour of the varied cultures of Spain.

One of the most famous buildings in the city is the Sagrada Familia Cathedral, designed by Barcelona's famous son, Antoni Gaudí. In fact, the city contains multiple examples of his unique style of architecture, which moulds stone into the shapes of Nature, but his most famous work is the Sagrada Familia, originally designed in 1883 but only partly built when Gaudí died in 1926. When I visited with my guests in the 1980s and 90s, we could only view the building from the outside since it was still under (very slow) construction – but I was fascinated by the sight of stone spires which seemed to melt like candle-wax as they reached down into the facades, twisting into the form of leafy branches. In 2016, I decided to return to Barcelona to explore parts of the city which I had never been able to visit with my guests. By this time, construction of the Sagrada Familia had progressed far enough that it was possible to walk inside (such a popular visit that it was necessary to book a strictly timed ticket, well in advance) ... a jaw-dropping experience! I was surrounded by sinuous columns soaring high into the roof above, as if I were standing in a dense forest, illuminated by a rainbow of vivid colours as sunlight poured through the huge stained glass windows. I would have liked to pause and drink in the scene, but was surrounded by milling hordes of tourists, most herded in tight groups by city guides who insisted that everyone kept moving – there seemed to be no quiet corner where I could stop and stare, unmolested.

When I visited Barcelona with my guests, I often told them about an entire city suburb created by Gaudí – Parc Gűell, but I had never had a chance to visit it. So, when I returned in 2016, I decided to explore it. It was not easy to reach (just as well I never tried to take my groups there), with a fairly long walk from the nearest metro station – though assisted by an impressive sequence of escalators and moving walkways to ease the steep climb to the hillside location. I was rather disappointed when I finally arrived, since I had not realised that this was a FAILED experiment by Gaudí to build a new type of community. He had intended to build 60 high quality and unique homes for the city's wealthiest citizens, but all he managed to create was an entrance flanked by lodges with fantastically shaped and coloured roofs, a terrace surrounded by a long stone bench decorated like a sea-serpent with mosaics of broken ceramic, and a series of roadways flying above pedestrian arcades, supported by columns shaped like the trunks of palm trees. I did not bother to buy a ticket to the Monumental Zone (which includes the terrace and entrance gate) since most of it was visible from the hill above ... instead I made my way up Gaudí's roadways to the rocky summit of the Park, where street entertainers and busking musicians were playing for the tourists as they relaxed and enjoyed the view over the city.

When I toured with my guests in the 1980s, it was easy to visit Barcelona without realising that it is actually a seaside city – the waterfront was lined with ugly warehouses and port installations. Then came the Summer Olympics of 1992, when the authorities opened up the seashore, creating a series of marinas (surrounded by luxurious cafes and restaurants), accessed by an elegant pedestrian bridge from the heart of the city, and by a cable-car strung from rickety iron towers, flying over the entire port before ascending Montjuic Hill. Montjuic is one of Barcelona's areas of green parkland, a refuge for the local people on hot summer days. It is also the location of the stark concrete Olympic Stadium and the Olympic swimming pools, with diving boards which look out over the entire city, 150m (500ft) below – surely a scary sight for the athletes as they prepare for their dives!

The Olympics encouraged the city authorities to open up several sandy beaches in the district of Barceloneta, mainly used by local people, who also flock to the picturesque beaches nestled in rocky coves north of Barcelona. In 2016, on the recommendation of several local residents, I took the local train as far as Blanes, the first resort at the start of the Costa Brava, boasting a broad strip of sandy beach backed by seafood restaurants and hotels, but not yet ruined by the tacky trappings of mass international 'beach tourism'. On the return journey, I stopped in the tiny resort of St Pol de Mar to explore its narrow alleyways lined with traditional, white-painted cottages, then decided to walk along the coastal footpath, taking the opportunity to enjoy the views over the rocky coastline. Approaching Calella, I was watching and photographing flocks of cormorants perched on the rocks above patches of sandy beach where sun-worshippers were soaking up the rays, when I suddenly realised that I could see more of those sunbathers than I might have expected: Calella is one of the locations along this coastline where nude bathing is permitted! Fortunately, most of the bodies were lying on their fronts … but still!

During my stay in Barcelona in 2016, I also took the opportunity to take a long day's tour into the nearby Pyrenees Mountains. We travelled by coach to the pretty town of Ripoli, clustered around the solid stone mass of a Romanesque monastery with a magnificent doorway carved in the 12th century. Equally attractive to us, however, at this first stop after an early start and a long drive, were the cafes serving a traditional breakfast of churros (doughnut fingers) dipped into thick hot chocolate! From Ripoli we continued by rack railway, winding between barren stony hillsides into the remote Nuria Valley where a tiny pilgrimage chapel sits on the shores of a lake, surrounded by 3000m (10,000ft) peaks. I took a cable car up towards the ski slopes, though of course there was no snow in August when I visited – instead, I found myself scrambling up very steep ski-pistes and, more frighteningly, slithering back down them: before setting off, I had not considered just how steep are the slopes which I would happily ski down when they are covered with snow! Yet my trek also allowed me to wander through alpine pastures thick with wild flowers and grazed by beautiful cattle, watching me in amazement from huge dark eyes with long eyelashes (these alpine Swiss Browns are just so attractive!).

I did not spend a lot of my working life on Spanish tours, since my company usually used specialists in the region, but several times I brought guests to Spain's capital, Madrid. I have never been a fan of big cities and was not particularly impressed with this one – a sprawling metropolis of massive stone buildings, dissected by wide avenues choked with traffic, though some roads were enlivened by fountains and there were several large city parks. During our visit, we travelled out to El Escorial, 40km (25mi) from Madrid – built in the 16th century as a combined monastery and royal palace by Philip II (the Spanish king who wanted to marry England's first Queen Elizabeth). He was a dour man who enjoyed living in the austere surroundings of this vast gloomy building – perhaps a lucky escape for Elizabeth? More interesting and impressive (to me), was an additional visit in the area, to the Valley of the Fallen, a huge memorial created by Franco to try to heal the wounds of the

Civil War. He ordered the construction of a massive underground crypt, carved into a rocky hillock topped by the largest stone cross in the world (150m/ 500ft high). Over 40,000 bodies of those who died in the Civil War, both Nationalist and Republican, were interred within the walls of the crypt. Franco himself was also buried there in 1975 and we saw his simple tomb – though in 2019 it was decided to exhume his body and rebury it in a private family grave, to stop any veneration of his dictatorship.

In 1992, my company organised a winter tour for its tour managers to Spain and Portugal – one of several occasions when they took us for an in-depth look at regions we would otherwise not have seen, sharing our in-house expertise amongst ourselves. For the first, and hopefully the last time in my life, I was taken into Gibraltar: a soul-less community which seems unable to decide whether it is Spanish or British, with tapas bars and red telephone boxes, outdoor markets and M&S stores – though of course there is also the iconic, soaring Rock of Gibraltar and its troublesome apes. Much more impressive are some of the centres of Moorish Spain, including Toledo – fortified on three sides by the deep rocky gorge of the River Tagus, and dominated by the massive 16th century fortress of Alcazar. It was once world-famous for the quality of its steel, used in swords and knives – today the souvenir shops mostly offer much tamer products like letter-openers! More of their influence can be seen in Seville, which was for a time the capital of Moorish Spain – its cathedral (the 3rd largest church in the world) was originally a mosque before being converted to a Catholic church in 1248, but now is dominated by massive golden altars, as well as the tomb of Christopher Columbus. My favourite corner of Seville is the Santa Cruz district, where narrow alleyways provide shade from the burning heat of the sun, and vivid window boxes provide splashes of colour. Even more interesting is the city of Granada, last stronghold of the Moors before they were driven out of Spain – dominated by the Alhambra Palace, a series of quadrangles where elegant rooms are open on one side, to face courtyards planted with lush gardens and cooled by fountains, tranquil pools and tinkling water-channels: all intended to create a 'paradise on earth'.

The most impressive Moorish city I have visited (on a separate occasion, travelling independently with no limits on my time) is Cordoba – once the capital of Moorish Al-Andalus. I arrived by train and trudged through extreme heat along avenues only partly shaded by orange trees, to the most famous building in the city – the Mezquita, a Moorish mosque later transformed into a Catholic cathedral. First sight was not inspiring – a forbidding fortress-like wall surmounted by a massive, square bell-tower. However, once I had passed through the grove of orange trees filling a patio where milling crowds of tourists were waiting for their guides to arrive with entry-tickets, I entered a dimly lit, cool forest of slim, elegant columns of marble, jasper and onyx, supporting a double row of red and white arches – like a vast forest reaching into the gloom, as far as the eye could see: the main prayer hall of the mosque. It was rather a shock to discover that part of the mosque had been demolished in the 16th century to insert a typically heavy Spanish-style cathedral decorated with fussy stucco and ornate gold-framed altarpieces – but it was easy to turn my back on that part of the building and to drink in the elegance of the Moorish structure, with its magnificent prayer niche (Mihrab) covered in intricate mosaic decoration and surmounted by a golden dome in the shape of a flower.

In Cordoba, I also saw traces of the ancient Roman occupation of Iberia – parts of the old town are still surrounded by Roman walls built in 206 BC, and a Roman bridge supported by immense buttresses, remained the only way to cross the River Guadalquivir for 2000 years and is still in use today. During our tour managers' 'educational trip' we were taken to see one of the best-preserved Roman structures in Spain – the aqueduct at Segovia. It was built in the 1st century AD and supplied all the city's water until the 19th century, still carrying water today. What an amazing structure – up to 28m (92ft) high at its highest point, supported by double arches of granite blocks held together without mortar … one of the most impressive Roman structures I have seen anywhere in Europe, yet unvisited by most European tours.

I came to know the far south of Spain fairly well once I started teaching tourism to college students. Each year, a colleague organised a week's trip to the Costa del Sol for a group of 16-year-olds, mixing the youthful attractions of Torremolinos and its raucous nightlife, with educational visits to tourist destinations in the area. We spent a day exploring the complex of dazzling, white-painted houses clustered around narrow alleyways in the town of Antequera, and nearby trekked between the weird, eroded rock pillars of El Torcal nature reserve – in places, resembling a lunar landscape. I usually 'brought up the rear', chivvying along students with ill-suited footwear, complaining bitterly about the unaccustomed physical exercise, instead of admiring the scenery! The students were generally much more content to visit Puerto Banus, an exclusive resort clustered around a harbour packed with luxury yachts – they often competed to see who could manage to get themselves photographed with a super-car, or even with its owner. On another day, we took the students to visit the resort of Nerja, admiring the view over a tiny patch of sand partially filled by beached fishing boats, from a specially built vantage point – the Balcón de Europa, then continuing into a series of show-caves just outside the town. We processed up and down stairways and concreted paths leading through passageways adorned with clusters of free-standing stalagmites and curtains of stalactites, into vast caverns. One is regularly used for concerts and houses a permanent stage and seating, whilst the most impressive is the Cataclysm Hall – over 100m (300ft) long and dominated by a central pillar standing 32m (105ft) high. Each time I visited, I was still impressed to emerge from a dark tunnel to find the path ahead dropping away on stairs into a vast dimly-lit cavern – the students were suitably awestruck!

On free days, when the students were generally sunning themselves on the beaches, my colleague and I would rent a car to explore a little further afield. On one occasion, we took ourselves to the picturesque town of Ronda, with its impressive bridge spanning the 120m (390ft) gorge of the Guadalevin River ... on another we visited the Camino del Rey pathway, built 1901-05 for workers to access the building site of a hydroelectric dam deep in the mountains. The path was just 1m (3ft) wide, constructed of concrete slabs resting on steel girders punched into the rock face, up to 100m (300ft) above the river. By the time we visited in the late 1990s, the path was deteriorating, with some of the handrails missing and holes appearing in the walkway. We picked our way cautiously along until we came to one of the places where the concrete had completely crumbled into the abyss ... bolder visitors were continuing to inch across on the steel beams, but we gave up at that point. A couple of years after our visit, several fatal accidents led to the path being closed to the public, but in 2014 reconstruction began and a new path, incorporating modern safety features, was opened in 2015 ... will I ever dare to traverse it, at some point in the future?

During my career in teaching, I was also lucky enough to escort several small groups of 17- and 18-year-old students financed by the European Erasmus Fund to spend a month in southern Spain, attending a language school in Malaga for a fortnight, then doing work experience in local tourism businesses. It was scary to be responsible for the students' well-being (quite different from escorting groups of adults on my coach tours) and there were several difficult situations – a case of severe sunburn, a student who felt uncomfortable and threatened in their work experience placement, students who over-indulged in drink during their free nights out on the town (I could not supervise them 24 hours a day!). However, we had a lot of fun helping each other to learn Spanish, with conversation hours in our hotel rooms, aided by stickers attached to a wide range of common objects, bearing their names in Spanish. Since our stay was always during the Easter holidays, I was delighted also to be able to take the students on the local train into Malaga to watch the traditional Easter parades: each day in Holy Week, 'brotherhoods' attached to different churches organise processions through the streets, wearing 'nazareno' costumes (penitential robes), including a conical hood which hides the wearer's face – very like the macabre costumes of America's Ku Klux Klan. Some of the penitents even flog themselves as they walk. The processions escort enormous wooden platforms adorned with gilded decorations, bearing more-than-life-size sculptures arranged to represent scenes from Christ's Passion, followed by smaller platforms bearing images of the Virgin Mary dressed in sumptuous robes and jewellery. Platforms weigh up to 5 tons and are carried on the shoulders of up to 270 bearers, grimacing from the effort, tightly packed shoulder to shoulder and swaying in unison as they walk through streets crowded with onlookers.

One region of Spain which I had never visited, was the north-west corner of the peninsula, so-called 'Green Spain', and the pilgrimage town of Santiago de Compostela … never visited, that is, until an unexpected addition to my cruise route, whilst returning to the UK from South America in January 2020. We had been due to sail direct from the Azores to London, but the captain received news of major storms in the Bay of Biscay and decided to extend the cruise by one day and wait for the storms to abate. He moored in the fishing port of Vigo, and offered an excursion by coach to Santiago … I jumped at the chance! We travelled past bays full of mussel and oyster beds, then through vineyards producing light, white Galician wines, before arriving in the city of Santiago de Compostela.

I was especially looking forward to seeing the world-famous pilgrimage church, built around the tomb of St James, patron saint of Spain. We had been warned that it was under renovation in preparation for a visit by the Pope in 2021 (though I imagine that visit was cancelled by the Covid pandemic), but had not anticipated quite how much renovation was taking place. We could not enter by the main doors, instead slipping through a side door via the museum, to find that the entire interior of the church was filled with a labyrinth of scaffolding poles and plastic sheeting – I am sure we should have been issued with helmets before entering! Normally, such major works would have demanded that the cathedral be closed entirely, but it forms the ultimate goal of one of the world's most popular pilgrimage trails, so it was essential that the pilgrims could at least access the sacred image of St James and his tomb. We were carefully ushered along a secured pathway through the labyrinth towards the main altar, where the face of St James peered at us between a maze of steel poles, then into the passageway behind the altar. The narrow steps led us up behind the statue, so that we could reach through to touch or kiss it, if we wished, then down underneath the altar to view the silver casket where the saint's bones are interred.

Though the visit to the cathedral was disappointing, the surrounding town was enchanting. I explored the granite-paved streets, lined with squat, stone buildings threaded by ancient arcades to shelter shoppers from the region's frequent rain showers. Then I adjourned to the historic pilgrims' hostel, founded in the 15th century to house pilgrims (and so considered the oldest hotel in the world), now an exclusive parador hotel which still offers a free meal to the first 10 pilgrims to arrive each day. Our tour included a coffee and snack in one of the ornate public rooms downstairs, but I managed to sneak away and explore the hotel's four interior courtyard gardens, and even to climb the stairs to see bedroom corridors accessed by vaulted stone doorways and the magnificent Royal Dining Room with panelled timber ceiling and chandeliers. If (when) I return to Santiago, perhaps I may lash out and stay a night in these elegant and historic surroundings?

PORTUGAL

I HAVE RARELY VISITED THIS small country – now almost a European backwater, though it is actually one of the oldest nations in Europe, established as an independent country in the 12th century, when it was reclaimed from the Moors and from the Spanish kingdoms. In the 15th and 16th centuries, the country was a major sea-power, with Portuguese navigators exploring and mapping the oceans and establishing a trading empire in Brazil, Africa, India and the Far East. Decline set in after a disastrous earthquake in Lisbon in 1755, and accelerated when Brazil claimed independence in 1822. In 1910, the monarchy was deposed and Portugal became a Republic, then from 1974 onwards their empire began to crumble – by 1999 Macau had been handed back to China, and East Timor was given independence in 2002. Today their only overseas territories are the Atlantic islands of Madeira and the Azores.

Though our tour managers' educational tour visited Lisbon, I have few memories of it. However, my cruise to South America in early 2020 stopped off for a night in Porto, and I elected to take an excursion to the important pilgrimage centre of Braga. Our guide told us that this city is incredibly proud of its position in Christian Iberia, since it was the site of the first archbishopric when Christianity reached the Roman community on the peninsula. It remained an unconquered focus of Christianity when the Muslim Moors occupied much of Iberia, and featured strongly in the Portuguese struggle to maintain independence from Spain in the 17th century. It is one of the most passionately Catholic cities in the country, with over 100 churches and chapels, and boasts the most impressive Holy Week parades in Portugal.

We followed a winding road, twisting through hills covered in eucalyptus forest to the outskirts of the town, where baroque-style churches perched on the top of various hills. We visited the most important of these sanctuaries, Bom Jesus, which sits at the top of a challenging zig-zag staircase climbing up the steep hillside on shallow steps set with a 'Portuguese pavement' – a mosaic of grey granite and white limestone laid in intricate patterns. At intervals, the stairs are flanked by pavilions housing 3-D scenes of the various stages of Christ's Passion – a traditional 'stations of the cross' route, though much more imposing than most, since the sculptures are each more than life-size. After visiting the sanctuary, we descended to the old town of Braga. The interesting part is relatively small, and rather run-down (perhaps awaiting an injection of money to restore it?), but there are some lovely palaces and city homes, many with facades of multi-coloured 'azulejo' tiles or painted stucco. At the heart of the old town stands the 11th century cathedral – a fairly small but very solid, granite church, built like a fortress. Inside, one end is very plain and restrained in décor, whilst the opposite end of the aisle bursts into a riot of 17th century baroque style – two huge, incredibly ornate organs rise into magnificently painted ceilings, drawing the eye upwards to two small jewels of modern stained glass. Once Covid allows, I would like to visit again and explore more of this fascinating town.

Portugal - Braga

FRANCE

MONACO

MANY OF OUR EUROPEAN TOURS travelled from Italy into France, passing en route the 2nd smallest country in Europe: the principality of Monaco (at less than $2.5km^2/1mile^2$, only the Vatican is smaller). Originally founded as a colony of Genoa, it was captured by the Grimaldi family in 1297 and has been ruled by the same family ever since – the current prince is Albert, the son of the Hollywood star Grace Kelly, who became Princess Grace of Monaco. Though it is an independent state, it is closely tied to France, uses French as its language and the Euro as its currency (though it is not a member of the EU). The state is largely financed by taxes on the many foreign businesses which have based themselves here because of low business rates – they pay enough for Monaco to avoid having to charge its residents income tax, which in turn has attracted huge numbers of wealthy foreigners to base themselves here (over 30% of the population are millionaires).

I regularly visited the state with my guests, walking through the narrow streets of the old town, perched high on its massive rock, to watch the elaborate (though at times bumbling) 'changing of the guard' ceremony outside the prince's palace (Monaco has an army of just 116 soldiers whose job is only to protect the prince and his palace – the defence of the country is in the hands of France). We also visited the cathedral, following a strictly enforced one-way system leading behind the altar to see the simple gravestone of Princess Grace, set into the floor and always adorned with fresh flowers. Later we moved to the harbourside community of Monte Carlo to visit glamorous Casino Square, filled with super-cars disgorging wealthy gamblers to disappear into private rooms at the back of the casino, whilst mundane tourists can only sip excessively expensive drinks in the Cafe de Paris or queue to enter the outer rooms of the casino, mainly taken up with slot machines. Everyone has to show their passports at the door to prove they are not Monegasque citizens, who are forbidden by law from gambling here. The third building around Casino Square is the luxurious Hotel de Paris – I sometimes set my guests the challenge of seeing whether they could get inside the hotel lobby: usually they were stopped by a vigilant concierge, skilled in the art of distinguishing the cream of society from the humdrum hoi-polloi like us, though occasionally one of my guests would triumphantly announce that they had made it! On one occasion, most of us managed to see a mysterious, white-gloved hand waving from an upstairs window – Michael Jackson was in town, staying in this most exclusive hotel.

There was never any question that we could take our coach up the narrow access road to the old town, perched on top of the rock at the heart of Monaco. When I first visited, the local police had a complex system of traffic management where our group left the coach at the bottom of the rock, to be shuttled uphill in special minibuses while our driver was ushered away to a parking lot some distance away – only to return when summoned by radio message from the policeman stationed at the drop-off point, to say that the group was awaiting pick-up (remember, back in the 1980s, there were no mobile phones). Finally, it became clear that something had to be done to improve the chaos as tourist numbers grew, and Monaco invested huge sums in hollowing multi-storey coach parks out of the rock, with huge elevators whisking tourists up to the heart of the old town – a really impressive example of tourism development, which worked remarkably well. For some years, we continued to be allowed to drop our guests at the side of the casino, returning at a set time to collect them again … but again the tourist numbers became unmanageable, so Monaco set up a new system, hiding the coaches away in the road tunnel beside the harbour and building more large lifts to carry visitors up to Casino Square – no expense spared!

Special memories of Monaco date from mid-winter tours which celebrated the New Year on the French Riviera. Since all the available restaurant parties were prohibitively expensive, I took my guests to a layby high on the cliffs above Monaco, providing sparkling wine and snacks to enjoy as we watched a magnificent midnight firework display provided (for free) by the state of Monaco. Guests visiting in May were able to watch as the city was transformed into a racetrack for the Formula One Grand Prix: clearing the inner harbour (for safety reasons) whilst the outer harbour filled with luxury yachts, some as big as small cruise ships; lining the roads with crash barriers; building grandstands and setting up pits for each team along the waterside. On one occasion, we were able to stroll in and out of the pits even as the mechanics were beginning to set up their machinery; on another occasion we almost got ourselves trapped in the city as the crash barriers made the bends on the exit roads so tight, that it was hard to manoeuvre the coach around them.

FRANCE

FRANCE IS THE LARGEST COUNTRY in western Europe, over twice the size of the UK, yet it has a population density less than half that of the UK – though it has some large cities, it is generally a sparsely populated, rural landscape. Unlike many European countries, it was unified under a single king (in more or less the same form as today) for almost 1000 years, with the most glamorous reign being that of the Sun King (Louis XIV) in the early 18th century. However, whilst the nobility lived in luxurious palaces like Versailles (outside Paris) or the magnificent chateaux in the Loire Valley, the majority of the French people existed in abject poverty – a situation which eventually led to the French Revolution, starting in 1789, when the king, queen and huge numbers of aristocrats were killed. The 19th century saw frequent changes of political regime, including the empire of Napoleon Bonaparte, which collapsed again when he was finally defeated in 1815 at Waterloo. Now it is settled as a republic under the leadership of a President.

For most of our guests, their first sight of France was in the French Riviera – one of the most beautiful areas in Europe. It offers beaches by the blue waters of the Mediterranean (though they are often quite narrow and partly closed off as the private property of high-class waterfront hotels), but within a short drive of the coast are the hills of the Maritime Alps, offering winter skiing and summer hiking. The summer climate is warm without usually being overpoweringly hot, and in winter it is mild with rarely any frost – ideal growing conditions for flowers; during our visits we often visited one of the perfume factories in Grasse, which use the mimosa, jasmine, roses and lavender which grow so abundantly in this region. After the sometimes run-down communities of Italy, Nice always seemed so well-maintained and colourful … unfortunately this impression caused my guests to relax their guard against the pickpockets which are prevalent in the tourist areas of Italy, but Nice has an equally large (if not larger) problem with casual thieving. I used to post one of my guests as a guard on the group's luggage whilst it sat on the pavement, waiting for porters to bring it inside the hotel, since it was not unknown for an opportunistic thief to rush past on a scooter and grab a suitcase in passing. I visited the police station in Nice as often as the one in Rome, helping guests to tearfully report the loss of valuables, money or (the biggest problem of all) passports – without travel documents, our guests could not enter another country (nor return home), so a stolen passport condemned them to hours spent in a consulate in Paris seeking temporary travel papers to allow them to leave France.

Away from Nice, there were rarely any problems, however, and my guests delighted in visits to some of the picturesque hilltop villages built centuries ago, when the region was under constant threat from marauding pirates. Now the winding cobbled streets of villages like Eze or St Paul de Vence, are lined with chic boutiques, flower-hung cafes offering tempting pastries, or artists' galleries selling paintings, sculptures or items carved from local olive wood. When I made an off-season visit with a rental car, I was able to explore the hinterland of Nice, ascending the dramatic hairpin bends of the Col de Braus into the mountains, and hiking among the idyllic lakes and hills of Mercantour National Park, close to the Italian border, where autumn had clothed the acres of larch trees in vibrant orange and yellow needles. Our tours provided a glimpse of these beautiful mountains as we headed north on a section of the Route Napoleon (used by the emperor in 1814 when he returned from his first exile in Elba, to try to rebuild his empire), following the River Var past the enchanting, fortified village of Entrevaux, perched on a hillside above the river and accessed only by a turreted medieval bridge. The road continued across the Col de la Croix Haute (1176m/ 3800ft), twisting and winding (causing sickness in some of my guests) through the French Alps. There were no handy service areas here for 'comfort stops' so morning coffee was taken in village cafés, where the ladies had to use a flat toilet basin (one group seemed unable to work out its use, until I gave a demonstration!), and lunch was a picnic in a flower-strewn meadow in the sunshine (or hunched miserably in the coach if it rained).

With some tours, we continued further east to the estuary of the River Rhone, settled by the ancient Romans from the 1st century BC until the collapse of their empire in the 5th century AD. They left behind some amazing structures, including the arenas in Arles and Nîmes (both smaller, but much better preserved than Rome's Colosseum) and the perfectly-preserved Maison Carrée, a gleaming white Roman temple in Nîmes. Perhaps most impressive is the Pont du Gard near Nîmes, an aqueduct 48m (160ft) high and 275m (900ft) long, built using stones so perfectly cut that they required no mortar to remain in place throughout its 2000-year history. On a trip organised by my tour company for its tour managers in the 1980s, to increase our knowledge of lesser-visited parts of France, we were taken to the atmospheric, semi-abandoned, medieval village of Les Baux, perched high on an eroded limestone rock, its houses partially carved into the rock and its cobbled streets winding up to a ruined fortress on the top of the rock. It was an eerie experience to walk the deserted streets, battered by typically strong winds – though sadly, the village has now been 'discovered' by mass tourism and, in season, over a million visitors are packed into the narrow alleyways, today lined with chic restaurants and craft shops.

We also visited the amazing caves of Lascaux in the Dordogne region, adorned with wall paintings believed to be 17,000 years old. The original caves were discovered in 1940 and opened to the public in 1948, but it was quickly realised that the heat and humidity from visitors was destroying the paintings, so the original caves were closed and replaced by replicas. On our visit we saw Lascaux II, a replica cave containing an exact copy of some of the finest animal drawings. We passed through a doorway into a gloomy subterranean chamber where subdued lighting illuminated images of magnificent long-horned cattle and tubby horses with small heads, outlined in black charcoal and then filled in with reddish iron oxide or yellow ochre.

Some were smaller than life-size, but others were huge – including a 5m (16ft) long bull. They galloped and leaped across the limestone walls, sometimes one set of animals drawn over a previous set – full of animation and energy. My visit was so long ago, but I will never forget the sense of awe which gripped me – though I was looking only at replicas, they were so authentic that I could imagine I was the very first explorer to see them.

At the mouth of the Rhone lie the salt-marshes of the Camargue district, an important refuge for migratory birds, where herds of white horses and black fighting bulls are tended by cowboys called 'gardiens'. On our tour managers' tour, we were taken out on horseback to explore the region: though it was an ideal way to experience this unique landscape, my main memory is of a horse which refused to respond to me and went its own steady way – I have no riding skills, and it clearly knew it! However, later I was able to share my new insights with guests, taking them to the quiet little town of Saintes-Maries-de-la-Mer with its imposing fortified church housing the relics of two of the 3 Marys who attended Christ's crucifixion and their dark-skinned servant Sara, patron saint of Romany gypsies. According to legend, this group of women was washed up here after their boat drifted away from the Holy Land after Christ's death, bringing Christianity to France. Now large pilgrimages make their way to this isolated town to celebrate the saints' holy days, most notably St Sara's festival in late May, which is attended by thousands of Romany gypsies.

Continuing westwards brought us to Carcassonne, an amazing medieval town built of golden stone, still entirely surrounded by massive walls. The walls were heavily (and not totally accurately) restored in the 19th century, so now there is a filmset quality about the 53 conical towers – in fact it is often used as a movie location, including for the film 'Robin Hood, Prince of Thieves' in 1991. Though the town is a major tourist attraction, I found it large enough to allow us to escape the crowds into narrow side-streets where normal life continues as it has for centuries – I was fascinated to see tiny grocery stores where it is still possible to buy a jugful of olive oil from huge barrels. Carcassonne sits close to the rugged Pyrenees Mountains which form the border between France and Spain. Deep in the mountainous foothills lies the pilgrimage centre of Lourdes, where a local girl (over 150 years ago) claimed a vision of the Virgin, revealing a healing spring of water to her. At first glance, the village seems tacky and overdeveloped, its streets lined with shops selling souvenir medals, plaster statues of the Virgin or overpriced plastic bottles which can be filled with sacred water. However, both my guests and I were impressed by the nightly Torchlight Procession through the town – large numbers of pilgrims carrying candles (provided for us by our hotel), reciting the Rosary and singing the Lourdes Hymn, each in their own language. Whether or not we believed in the healing power of the spring, it was impossible not to be moved by the intense devotion of so many pilgrims and the sight of thousands of tiny flames moving through the darkened streets.

Central France is the location of many of the famous wine regions. At the mouth of the River Garonne sits the elegantly imposing city of Bordeaux, transformed in the 18th century by monumental town houses and mansions, whilst in the midst of its hinterland of vineyards sits the enchanting village of St Emilion, with picturesque streets winding between ancient stone-built houses and squat Romanesque churches (including the underground Monolithic Church, carved in the 12th century from a single massive rock). Further east lies the Burgundy region, where my tours often stopped in Beaune for wine-tasting in one of the many cellars clustered around the picturesque 15th century Hotel Dieu, with its colourfully patterned tile roof. On the boundary of France and Germany lies the Alsace region, where vineyards producing a German-style white wine nestle in the foothills of the thickly forested Vosges Mountains: the picturesque town of Colmar is filled with medieval half-timbered houses which also seem more German than French (but then, Alsace is a region alternately snatched by Germany and France over the centuries, so perhaps it is inevitable that the two cultures will be blurred). On some of my earliest tours, we passed through the Champagne vineyards, lying to the east of Paris – but those high-speed itineraries allowed no time for sampling the vintage!

One of the highlights of central France is the Loire Valley, which became the favourite residence of the 16th century king Francis I – for a time, the most powerful sovereign in Christendom and a great rival of the English king Henry VIII. Since the king was living here, the nobility of France followed him, buying up the ruins of former fortresses and converting them into Renaissance-style chateaux – there are 300 castles in the area, ranging from ancient fortresses to luxurious palaces. King Francis built grand palaces in both Blois and Amboise, and also a 'hunting lodge' at Chambord – not really a 'lodge', since it is the largest chateau in the Loire Valley, famous for a roofline studded with 365 chimneys, and for a magnificent double-spiral staircase (supposedly designed by Leonardo da Vinci, who had been invited by Francis I to spend the last years of his life in France). Though this is the most famous chateau in the region, I preferred the much smaller chateau of Chenonceau, built in the form of a bridge across the little River Cher – given as a gift by King Francis' son Henry to his mistress Diane, but spitefully seized by his widow Catherine after Henry's sudden death in a jousting accident. Both these ladies spent large sums on beautifying the palace and creating splendid formal gardens on the river bank. Even more entrancing is the little chateau of Azay-le-Rideau, perched on an island in the centre of the River Indre, its ornate fortifications reflected in the tranquil water around it. Many of the Loire chateaux which are open to the public, are unfurnished (the French Revolution and successive wars stripped them of their treasures) but in Azay-le-Rideau there has been an attempt to refurnish the rooms as they would have been over successive generations of owners.

Now to Paris, highlight of every European tour: I am not usually fond of big cities, but Paris is something special. Unlike many European cities, it was untouched by the wars of the 20th century – the fighting of World War 1 did not (quite) reach it, and in World War 2 it was declared an open city, protected from damage so long as there was no military action there. Consequently, the extensive city centre is still filled with magnificent buildings constructed over the many centuries since Paris became capital of France. The Louvre Palace represents this beautifully: originally a medieval fortress; transformed into a royal palace in the 14th century; rebuilt by successive monarchs over the 16th and 17th centuries into the form it has today; its courtyard cleared in the 19th century to make room for a mini Arc de Triomphe; a modernistic glass pyramid added in 1989 to form the entrance of today's Museum. Unlike London, where the generations of buildings are jumbled together, Paris was always developed under the scrutiny of the French kings; standing on the Trocadéro Square, I could lead my guests' eyes past the 20th century Chaillot Palace to the 19th century Eiffel Tower and on to the 18th century Military School – all fitting together into one unbroken panorama. I love the fact that the city is continuing to add more splendid structures to its hoard, celebrating its past but also rejoicing in its future.

My guests were always entranced with the city, especially when they joined me on their very first evening for a tour of the illuminations – few cities succeed as well as Paris in lighting their monuments by night. We started at the 13th century Notre Dame Cathedral, where the lights cast a mysterious shadow (uncannily like Victor Hugo's Hunchback) on to the facade – will he still be visible, when the cathedral is finally restored after the terrible fire in 2019? We followed the Seine River westwards past the medieval Conciergerie fortress which became an infamous prison, where Queen Marie Antoinette spent her last days, then drove into the vast Concorde Square where she was beheaded in the French Revolution. The Champs Élysées boulevard is especially beautiful when its trees are garlanded with lights at Christmas, and Napoleon's huge Arc de Triomphe is most impressive by night when it is possible to glimpse the flickering of the Eternal Flame beneath its arches. By night the traffic is light enough to allow a coach to circle the Arch a few times – in the daytime it is a nightmare drive, with 12 avenues opening into a single roundabout … and priority given to those entering the flow of traffic, rather than to those leaving it. On one memorable winter tour, escorting a group of Australian schoolgirls, they pleaded to be allowed to see in the New Year among the crowds at the Arc de Triomphe: we parked as close as possible and they rushed off excitedly, only to return a short time later, exclaiming in disgust "those sleazy Frenchmen wanted to kiss us" – not understanding that a kiss is a normal greeting in France. A reminder that there are many differences in 'normal behaviour' between the countries of the world!

Our illumination tour finished at the Eiffel Tower – unimpressive when I first visited Paris in the 1970s, since the floodlights at ground level were unable to illuminate its full 300m (almost 1000 ft) height … then in 1985, sodium lights were installed inside the entire structure, giving it a golden sheen by night. What a surprise to me when I brought my first guests of the year to see the Tower – I had not realised that its lighting had been changed. Just as I conducted my last tours to Paris in 2000, there was another change – thousands of individual flashing bulbs were added, so that for 10 minutes in each hour (now reduced to just 5 minutes) the entire Tower glitters.

Paris by day could not rival the city by night, but there were highlights which brought a communal gasp of admiration from my groups: walking into Notre Dame Cathedral on a sunny day to find the stained glass in the twin rose windows has filled the nave with coloured patterns ... entering the Sainte Chapelle as if walking into a jewel box, its richly decorated, vaulted ceiling supported only by slim stone columns, since the rest of the walls are filled with glorious stained glass windows ... riding the Eiffel Tower's elevator, with vertiginous views down to the ground, supported only by apparently flimsy steel girders ... trying to understand the complex, inside-out structure of the Pompidou Centre, with coloured pipes carrying water and electricity, and a snaking covered escalator, all hung from the outside of the steel scaffolding which supports the exhibition halls ... riding seemingly endless escalators which plunge deep into the underground shopping complex of Les Halles. And, of course, there was always a nervous giggle as we drove through the streets of Pigalle, full of peep-shows and shops selling sex aids, past the massive (if rather shabby by day) red windmill marking the Moulin Rouge cabaret club. Occasionally I took guests to see the expensive show at the Moulin Rouge, or the even more expensive show at the Lido – but usually I preferred to offer the cheaper performance at the Nouvelle Eve, where the standard of speciality acts was just as good, though the lines of high-kicking girls (dressed in little more than a few feathers) were shorter.

Normally we spent two nights in Paris, with the second night devoted to a Farewell Dinner in a typical Parisian brasserie – however, occasionally my tours remained for three nights. I was keen that my guests should seek out a restaurant for themselves on that extra night, to make a special memory of their own, though it turned into a nightmare for one group I escorted – a group made up entirely of New Zealanders from quiet rural towns in South Island. They had stuck faithfully to me throughout their month-long tour, trusting my recommendations implicitly, and they were terrified to be sent out into Paris to find their own dinner. Most ended up in the hotel restaurant, unable to understand the French menu – the only word they recognised was 'steak', so they all chose that dish. Unfortunately it was actually 'steak tartare' – and the one thing which rural New Zealanders will not eat, is raw meat! Oh dear!

West of Paris lie the beaches used by soldiers in the Normandy Landings on 6th June 1944, which turned the course of WW2. The little town of

Arromanches has established itself as a centre for those visiting these sites, with a museum offering photographs and models. Otherwise this coastline is quiet and little-visited, a region of wide sandy beaches where abandoned tanks adorn war memorials and unremarkable lumps of concrete, once fortifications, are still scattered across the landscape. A few large cemeteries contain the graves of fallen soldiers gathered from different WW2 battlefields. On the other hand, northern France is littered with tiny walled cemeteries from WW1, each guarded by a tall white cross – the land is full of memories of the tragedies of this war, when vast areas of land were constantly pounded by heavy bombardment which destroyed villages and farmland, as well as killing untold numbers of soldiers. On some tours, we turned aside from our journey back to Calais, to visit the Canadian memorial at Vimy Ridge, surrounded still by preserved trenches and shell-holes. However, my first introduction to the horrors of WW1 was further east at Verdun, where the battle (fought February to October 1916) was probably the French army's most bitter conflict in the entire war, with an estimated 362,000 men killed. It was seen as vital for the safety of Paris that Verdun should not fall, so the French poured in more and more troops for 300 days – now the whole area is a memorial, still littered with shell-holes grown over with grass and trees. At its heart is the Ossuary of Douaumont where the bones of unidentified soldiers, both French and German, are piled together behind small windows which make them visible to visitors: the remains of at least 130,000 men – and alongside is a cemetery with the identified graves of over 16,000 soldiers. Though I have never returned to Verdun after completing a series of tours in the 1970s, I will not forget the shock of seeing evidence of such huge loss of life, right before my own eyes.

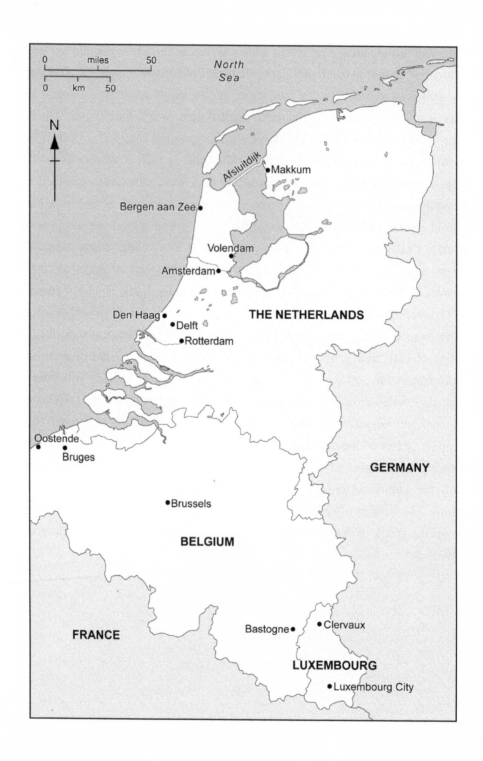

THE LOW COUNTRIES

BELGIUM

FOR MANY OF MY GUESTS, Belgium was a country simply to be rushed through on smooth motorways leading to other parts of Europe, but in my earliest years as a tour manager (in the 1970s) I conducted tours which spent time in various parts of the country. It is one of Europe's smaller countries, just 1½ times the size of Wales, but with 4 times the population – a densely populated land. It is also one of Europe's newer countries, formed only in 1830 when, after hundreds of years of wars between France and the Netherlands, it was constructed out of a section of each of those two countries (with a small piece of Germany annexed after WW1), taking a German prince as their first king, Leopold. Perhaps it is inevitable that there is still considerable tension between French-speaking Belgians (Walloons) and Dutch-speaking Belgians (Flemish), only partially resolved when they moved to a federal government in 1993.

In the 1970s, my tour groups reached Europe by ferry into Oostende from Dover (a 4-hour route which has now been suspended), discharging hundreds of passengers at a time on to the quay where up to 40 coaches were parked, leaving them wandering aimlessly seeking the correct coach. Inevitably there were some passengers who boarded the wrong vehicle, so my first task was to check that everyone on board was actually intending to travel on my tour – if necessary, politely pointing them instead to the correct coach. If I was missing one of my guests, I had to visit all the other nearby coaches, calling out their name to see if they had boarded the wrong vehicle. On one occasion, I rescued one of my guests from another coach, without realising that he had already loaded his luggage there – he enjoyed a 14-day tour of eastern Europe, whilst his luggage toured Scandinavia for 14 days: they were only reunited in the baggage hall back at Dover. At least they were re-united … in the days before roll-on/roll-off ferries, each group's baggage was swung out of the ship's hold in cargo nets, and I watched in horror as a suitcase slipped from the net holding our baggage, splashing into the sea – I could not bring myself to tell my guest that his luggage was lost at sea, so instead re-assured him that he would probably find it waiting for him when he returned to the UK. In all these situations, the first stop we made was at a shopping complex, so the guest could buy emergency supplies (paid for by travel insurance) – it is amazing how little baggage a traveller actually needs!

One of the prettiest towns in Belgium is Bruges (called Brugge by native Flemings), its entire civic centre declared a UNESCO World Heritage site in 2000. The town blossomed for 400 years from the 12th century, with a sheltered inlet allowing traders into the heart of the community, attracting merchant fleets from all over Europe. Canals were dug to give easy access to all parts of the town, and wealthy merchants built splendid brick mansions with gabled facades, and churches with massive towers and spires. In the early 16th century, the sea-inlet began to silt up so that trading ships could no longer navigate it … trade moved instead to nearby Antwerp, and Bruges was left in a time-warp, ignored by the outside world until tourism began in the 19th century. It was virtually undamaged in both World Wars, and so today offers one of the best-preserved medieval town centres in Europe. It is sometimes called the 'Venice of the North' because of its canals – though there is no comparison with the real Venice, since there are roads alongside the canals everywhere.

For our sightseeing walk, our driver was permitted to drop us in the Market Square at the heart of the town (though he then had to drive away to park elsewhere), after I had repeated again and again that my guests MUST return on time, since the coach could not stop to pick us up for longer than a few minutes. In those days, we had no mobile phones which would have permitted me to call up the driver once the whole group was assembled – we had to rely on the punctuality of the group and of the driver, to make contact at precisely the same moment. Fortunately, it was rare that guests got lost in Bruges, since the Market Square is dominated by the massive Belfry Tower (visible from every part of the town centre). Official sightseeing usually consisted only of a walk through the picturesque streets – there was no time even to take a cruise on the canals, never mind to visit one of the most magnificent churches in town: the Basilica of the Holy Blood. However, on a private visit one winter, I finally managed to see it – finding a glorious double chapel with an elaborately carved stone facade adorned with golden statues. The lower chapel is a dark, sombre, yet peaceful 12th century structure with bare brick walls, whilst the upper part was rebuilt in the 16th century in soaring Gothic style – a barrel roof supported by delicate columns either side of massive stained glass windows which flood the chapel with light. Every inch of the walls is painted with frescoes – a feast for the eyes! Our official sightseeing did, however, find time to visit the Beguinage, originally built for a community of pious single or widowed women, but now occupied by Benedictine nuns. We entered through a gatehouse, plunging immediately into the deep tranquility of a garden with wide lawns (dotted with daffodils in spring) planted with shady trees, surrounded by clusters of white-painted houses. In the streets around, we often saw local ladies sitting in their doorways with lace-cushions on their knees, producing the fine lace for which the town is famous.

On a few tours, we stayed in the Belgian capital, Brussels – a large and relatively uninteresting city, with just a few notable highlights. In the leafy suburb of Laken stands the Atomium, a weird structure in the form of a vastly magnified molecule of iron – a complex of balls and tubes in gleaming stainless steel (made in Sheffield), towering 102m (335ft) above the ground. Even as an inexperienced tour manager, it was easy to find the Atomium, but the same cannot be said of Brussels Cathedral. Part of my duties included conducting an evening tour of the city's highlights for my guests, though I had never been to Brussels before … all I had to assist me was a map and a sheaf of information I had researched in advance, plus a driver who (fortunately) knew his way around the city. On my first ever visit, I was doing fairly well at anticipating the next 'sight' to appear and giving appropriate information before we arrived. Next destination was the cathedral, according to my map, so I peered ahead and glimpsed a church – time to start recounting its story. However, as we came closer, I realised that this church was dirty, covered with graffiti and apparently abandoned ... I informed my guests that it was 'under renovation'. Then we turned a corner and there was Brussels Cathedral – a massive Gothic edifice with imposing twin towers, similar to Notre Dame in Paris ... I had to admit to my guests that I had made a mistake!

In a little backstreet in the heart of the city, sits perhaps the most famous sight of Brussels – the Mannekin Pis fountain. My guests always wondered why I was leading them down an uninteresting street of offices and parking garages, until we reached the street corner where this tiny statue of a young boy stands, with water running from ... well, you can guess where! Nearby lies the Grand Place, a medieval square enhanced by soft golden lighting in the evenings. The oldest building on the square is the 15th century Town Hall, built at the time when the merchant classes were growing in influence, to equal the power of the ruling dukes – its elaborate facade is dominated by a massive, if out-of-proportion, tower. In response to the challenge of the Town Hall, in the 16th century the dukes built the so-called King's House (though no king ever lived there) on the opposite side of the square – an even more elaborate confection of arches and spires, but not as large or imposing as the Town Hall. The 'battle' for prestige was won by the merchants, who then surrounded the rest of the square with opulent gabled guildhouses decorated with gold leaf.

Explaining the architecture of the Grand Place to my guests was not difficult ... except on one occasion when we finally arrived in Brussels after a nightmare winter journey. We were travelling north from Austria, when we became stuck in heavy snow on the German motorways – my guests slept in their seats, but I kept myself from sleep throughout the night to help the driver to stay awake. We reached our overnight hotel in Germany at breakfast time and were permitted by the hotel to rest in our allocated rooms only for several hours, before we had to continue to our next overnight stop in Brussels – missing all the included sightseeing stops along the way, so that we reached the hotel by early evening. The driver went straight to his room, but I felt I should try to ensure the guests did not miss any more of the highlights of their tour, so we set out to walk from the hotel to the Grand

Place. Unfortunately, when we arrived, I was so tired that I could not find any words to explain the buildings to my guests. However, this group was so kind and understanding ... several of them quickly invented a colourful story of their own about the architecture they were seeing, and then packed me off to bed!

My personal memories of Brussels will always include the hotel where we stayed in the 1970s – scene of a few unforgettable events, which fortunately I did not experience for myself. A colleague told me that her tour had spent their first night there, to find next morning that one of the group (a newly-married Indian girl) had disappeared. Her husband did not seem concerned and continued with the tour as normal – but later the dismembered body of his bride was found in the hotel's waste system ... who knows what tragedy occurred on the first night of their honeymoon? The same hotel, a few years later, was partly damaged by a fire (apparently caused by Chinese tourists lighting a stove to cook food in their room) which killed several guests (including a tour manager working for a rival company). I stayed in the hotel again soon afterwards, curiously opening a new door which had appeared to block off part of the corridor – beyond it, the walls were still charred from the fire ... but the hotel continued to accept bookings for the rest of the summer season, only closing for repairs when the winter season arrived.

I rarely visited the southern, French-speaking part of Belgium, except as an overnight stop on a long transfer back to the Channel ports from a residential stay in Austria – a regular journey which I undertook in the very hot summer of 1976. We had no air-conditioning in the coaches, back in those days, so my guests were always stressed and irritable after a broiling day on the road, ventilated only by judicious use of the emergency hatches in the coach roof. We passed Bastogne, site of a week-long siege in WW2, when American troops were trapped in the town until rescued by the advance of General Patton's 3rd Army. We also passed Mons, where the British army fought their first battle of WW1 before they were forced to retreat, leaving the town occupied by Germans until the end of the war ... a plaque in the town claims "Here was fired the last shot of the Great War". However, there was no time to visit either of these sites – my focus was simply on completing the journey and returning the group to the Channel ferries. All I really remember of my visits to Wallonie (southern Belgium) is again our hotel – a damp, smelly motel which none of us enjoyed. On one occasion a guest came to me in distress as we left the motel, claiming that her (very expensive) engagement ring had gone missing – perhaps stolen by hotel staff. We had a ferry to catch ... I could not delay our departure to bring in the police, and the guest was not willing to be left behind to contact the police on her own, so I simply wrote out a confirmation for her insurance company that the ring had been lost. However, hours later, another guest took me aside to tell me that they had never seen the lady wearing an engagement ring – had I been duped? Did the insurance company cough up the money? I never heard any more – but the situation certainly contributed to making me a more experienced tour manager!

LUXEMBOURG

LUXEMBOURG IS ANOTHER OF EUROPE'S 'mini-states' (with an area of 2500 km^2 /1000 miles^2), but it definitely punches above its weight diplomatically, since it was a founder member of the Benelux union (which later expanded into the European Union) and its capital is one of the four official capitals of the EU (together with Brussels, Strasbourg and Frankfurt), home of the European Court of Justice and the European Investment Bank. It is ruled as a constitutional monarchy by a Grand Duke and is one of the richest countries in Europe, with a thriving financial and banking sector. The people are generally tri-lingual, with French and German used as administrative languages, whilst at home they speak Luxembourgish (a Germanic language with frequent hints of French).

When I first started my career as a tour manager, my employers usually allocated a single itinerary for me to escort throughout the season. In my first year (1975), that itinerary was the 'Five European Capitals' – one of our so-called Pyjama Tours (which moved so fast that there was barely time to change out of our pyjamas!). In just one week, we moved from Brussels to Amsterdam to Bonn (at the time, western capital of a divided Germany) to Paris – but there was just time to squeeze in one more capital, Luxembourg City. This was once one of the strongest fortifications in Europe, built around deep gorges cut by the Alzette and Petrusse Rivers, the cliffs of the gorges honeycombed by a vast tunnel network called the Casemates. Our sightseeing tour took us back and forth across several impressive bridges to see ponderous buildings housing the European institutions – however, my guests were most impressed by tree-lined promenades offering dramatic viewpoints over the gorges.

My own memories of the city are mostly dominated (again!) by an unpleasant hotel. This one usually allocated me a room located directly between the two parallel lift shafts (the noise of the lifts persisted throughout the night), so narrow that there was no space for a suitcase – I had to unpack what I needed for the night while my case sat on my bed, then put the suitcase outside the door so that I could access the bed myself. On one visit, this hotel told me that I would have to send some of my guests to an annexe: I had a family group of Israelis travelling with me, so thought they could support each other in a different building better than some of my individual guests. Unfortunately, the 'annexe' turned out to be a brothel. When they returned to the original hotel for dinner, one of the family was so angry that he threatened me with a knife, accusing me of being prejudiced against Israelis!

This particular group was one of the most difficult I have ever escorted, containing over 20 different nationalities: Arabs as well as Israelis; Pakistanis and Indians; Japanese and Indonesians who spoke only minimal English; francophone Canadians who preferred to speak French. There was also a white South African girl whose first request to me, was not to be accommodated with a black person (this was still the time of the apartheid regime). However, the only possible female to share her room was a Sri Lankan girl ... and they quickly became best friends. The South African girl said to me at the end of the tour, "No-one ever told me that they are just the same as us": one of the most treasured moments of my career – tourism CAN be a force for good!

Some years later I returned to Luxembourg for an off-season break, exploring especially the thickly forested region known as 'Luxembourg Switzerland', cut by peaceful river valleys dotted with picturesque villages. Further north, I visited the little town of Clervaux, nestled deep in a hidden valley, dominated by an imposing 12th century castle which was badly damaged in WW2 and was only partially restored when I visited, but now it is open to the public as a museum. I was impressed on my brief visit by the rural and peaceful landscape, but have not yet managed to return to explore further.

THE NETHERLANDS

IN BRITAIN, THIS COUNTRY IS often called Holland – but that actually refers to just two of their 12 provinces, North and South Holland (in the west of the country). The correct name (the 'Netherlands', meaning the 'Low Countries') accurately describes the landscape: only 50% of the country is over 1m (3ft) above sea-level, and 26% is even below sea-level – vast areas of reclaimed land called 'polders', many of them originally drained by the famous windmills, though now maintained by modern pumps. If you go back into history, the western regions were no more than marshy river estuaries with villages or farms perched on man-made hillocks, constantly threatened by flooding – the last major floods were in 1953: a disaster which led to a system of water-control measures called the Delta Works, considered one of the wonders of the modern world. Historically, farming was difficult because of the risk of flooding, so instead the people turned to trading to make a living. Especially in the 17th century, merchant seamen sought out new trade routes all over the world, exploring the seas around Australia and New Zealand, establishing trading ports wherever they went, even building an empire including much of the East Indies (now Indonesia), southern India and Africa – several Caribbean Islands are still part of the Netherlands. Today, they have developed an intensive style of agriculture (including many acres under glass), so that the Netherlands is the 2nd largest exporter of food and agricultural products in the world.

In the 1970s, I came to know the north-western part of the country very well, spending several months a year conducting 'Bulb Tours' – back-to-back short tours which spent a day travelling around the region seeking bulbfields still bearing flowers (frustratingly, the growers de-head the plants as soon as the daffodils, hyacinths or tulips come into bloom, to preserve the strength of the bulb – the main product). We also explored the Keukenhof Gardens, planted afresh each year by the growers to showcase their finest spring-flowering varieties, then continued to visit some of the historic towns in South Holland: picturesque Delft, with gabled houses lining narrow canals, where the famous blue & white pottery is produced; seaside Scheveningen (where we stopped at the fishing harbour for my guests to sample raw herring); Den

Haag (the Hague), seat of the national government in the historic 13th century courtyards of the Binnenhof Palace, and workplace of the monarch in the nearby Noordeinde Palace. Sometimes we visited the ancient town of Gouda, famous for cheese, but also for pottery featuring brightly coloured designs on a dark background ... and my guests insisted that we also visit the tiny village of Edam, though there was little to see there except pleasant tree-lined waterways and small but immaculate houses – in the polders of the Netherlands, there is little land suitable for building (often construction is only possible once long concrete-capped wooden pilings have been driven into the ground as a foundation), making land too expensive for more than the smallest of houses.

Our Bulb Tours often stayed in North Holland, in the fishing village of Volendam, a cluster of tiny homes (the fishing community was originally very poor) hidden behind a high dam which holds back the water of the Ijsselmeer lake – to reach our hotel, the coach had to negotiate the narrow, cobbled street on top of the dike. My guests were always delighted with this hotel, a sprawling wooden building in the heart of the village, still decorated inside with nautical memorabilia on the walls and traditional finely-woven carpets on the tables. Though the village was busy with visiting tourists during the day, in the early mornings our hotel was still the meeting place of local fishermen, wearing their thick, baggy, woollen trousers and functional clogs. A few years ago, I returned to Volendam for a short visit, but was shocked to discover how much tourism has grown over the years – now the main street is so clogged with strolling visitors that it is impossible for vehicles to access the hotel except in the evenings, and coaches can never reach it. The hotel has been transformed into chic boutique accommodation (the tiny attic room where I was accommodated, at the top of a ladder-like wooden staircase, has disappeared), and the only trace of a fishing industry is in the harbourside booths selling smoked eel. However, at least tourism has preserved one of Volendam's traditions – many of the waitresses and shop assistants wear the local costume: a long, striped apron, embroidered chestpiece and high pointed bonnet. Across the water from Volendam lies Marken, once an even poorer fishing village of green & white wooden houses located on a former island. When we visited in the 1970s, there were still a few elderly ladies wearing their traditional costumes every day: a full dark skirt and an embroidered corset with a plain white cap. These ladies also still sported the traditional Marken haircut – a pair of long curly locks framing their face, while the back of their heads was shaved. By the time I returned in 2014, these ladies were long gone and I saw no sign of traditional costume, even in the tourist facilities. Gone too, was the opportunity to visit one of the houses with an elderly lady who proudly explained that she had raised 11 children in her one-up/ two-down cottage – the parents slept in a cupboard-bed in the living room along with the latest baby, while all the other children packed themselves into the upstairs room!

Further north lies the resort of Bergen aan Zee, where I attended a short language course during my university studies in 1971. How discouraging, when I was attempting to learn Dutch, to be corrected in my pronunciation even by a local bus driver, speaking perfect English. I was to learn, over my years of visiting the country, that most Dutch people speak excellent English (perhaps from watching American TV programmes, normally sub-titled instead of dubbed) – though they were always delighted to find that someone had troubled to learn their language. The entire Dutch coast is lined with a thick band of sand dunes (part of their sea-defences) leading to long, empty sandy beaches – as young students, we did not hesitate to take a midnight dip in the sea at Bergen, finding the water filled with fluorescent organisms which made us glow as we emerged from our swim. When I re-visited in 2014, I still found the same long empty beaches and windswept, isolated dunes – but was not tempted to swim!

Closing off the former Zuiderzee is the Afsluitdijk, a 32km (20 mi) long dike which holds back the North Sea and, since its construction in 1932, has allowed the formation of the freshwater Ijsselmeer. It is a weird feeling as you drive across, as if you are on an unending track leading out into the ocean with gulls soaring beside you … and ocean winds battering you. On our Bulb Tours, we crossed the dike to reach the small port of Makkum – not an especially pretty village (especially when compared to other historic Zuiderzee ports like Hoorn or Enkhuizen), but memorable for the feast which a restaurant laid on for my guests … a vast 'koffietafel' consisting of many different types of bread (including delicious currant bread), cheeses, cold meats, salads and pastries, all served with unlimited coffee or tea. One of the best meals of the tour, my guests said. Buffets seem popular with the Dutch, since their other 'typical' meal is the Indonesian 'rijstafel' – a parade of up to 40 dishes filled with differently flavoured and textured foods (spicy, savoury and sweet) accompanied by rice.

Most European tours which visit the Netherlands, concentrate only on exploring the city of Amsterdam – a former fishing village which rose to become one of the most important ports in the world during the Netherlands' 17th century Golden Age. Its main attractions are the concentric, hand-dug rings of canals which both protected the wealthy heart of the city and also provided easy transportation from the port to the merchants' warehouses. Alongside the waterways are the grand mansions of rich traders, topped by soaring gables and accessed always by flights of steps – the more steps to reach the front door, the more prestige claimed by the resident. However, only the wealthiest of all could afford the ultimate luxury – floor-space! With the ground really too soft for building, it was a major engineering exercise to build these houses – so they were built tall and narrow, to take up as little land as possible. Inside, each storey is accessed by stairways so narrow and steep that it is virtually impossible to carry furnishings upstairs … so most buildings have a beam projecting from the gable, from which a block and tackle can be rigged to lift large items and take them in through a window on the appropriate floor. As they cruised the canals in glass-topped boats, my guests were always thrilled to watch a grand piano or double bed being hoisted into place!

On every tour, we took guests into a diamond factory for an explanation of the grading system for these gems, a glimpse of a workman painstakingly cutting a raw stone … and the chance to purchase a piece of jewellery. Whilst conducting Bulb Tours, I brought hundreds of groups to these salerooms, and surprisingly they often bought a diamond – eventually the factory allowed me to choose a tiny ring for myself without payment: I gave it to my mother. On some tours, there was time for guests to visit one of the city's art galleries – most popular being the Rijksmuseum's displays of works by Rembrandt and Vermeer, and the nearby Van Gogh museum. Occasionally there was time to explore some of the hidden corners of the city – I especially enjoyed visiting the floating flower market (a string of flower shops located on barges along one of the canals) or the Begijnhof – a hidden garden in the oldest part of the city, entered through a fortified gateway and surrounded by gabled houses once occupied by Beguines (pious older ladies who lived almost as nuns) but now home to 105 single ladies. Later in my career, when I worked for a company which gave me more flexibility in the excursions I could offer to my guests, I was able to drive them out to visit the huge Aalsmeer flower markets on the outskirts of Amsterdam. It is a fully commercial operation, but adapted to allow tourist access – a raised walkway took us over the market area, watching as automatic electric carts scurried across the warehouse floor below us, shuttling trolley-loads of flowers from different growers into one of several auction rooms. We could watch the action in the auction rooms too, from behind glass so that we did not distract the proceedings as rows of bidders focused on a 'clock' showing a swiftly descending price for each trolley, pushing a button to stop the clock when it reached the price they were willing to pay ... fascinating to watch!

On every tour, I had requests from my guests to be taken to the infamous Red Light district. When I was visiting in the late 20th century, prostitution was tolerated and regulated in the Netherlands ... since 1999 it is fully legalised, so that girls can equip themselves with heated and sanitary premises to carry on their 'work' – each one fronted by a 'shop-window' where the girls can display themselves. A red light illuminated above the window means the girl is 'on duty'; if the curtain is drawn across the window, she is busy. There is a network of canal streets close to the heart of the city, where these 'shops' are located, and groups of gawking tourists are normally tolerated so long as they do not dawdle or mock the girls, and especially do not try to take photographs. Sometimes we would find that the girls swiftly disappeared into the rear of their premises as we approached, unless there was also a potential client looking inside – so I suggested that several of my more likely male customers walked ahead of us, so there were still a few girls for the rest of the group to see. However, there was one notable occasion when we started our walk and I could immediately feel a tension in the air ... we continued walking for a short time, until a policeman appeared ahead of us, ordering us into a side-alley leading away from the Red Light district. Apparently there had been some trouble in the previous hours and it was not safe to walk through on this evening.

The second city of the Netherlands is Rotterdam, Europe's largest seaport – though most of the modern port lies between the city and the mouth of the River

Maas (a branch of the mighty Rhine) on which it stands. Before WW2, this was another historic city like Amsterdam, but on the night of the 14th May 1940 it was bombed out of existence by the German Luftwaffe, to hasten the capitulation of the Netherlands to invading German forces. I had occasionally driven through the city, usually en route from the ferryport at Hoek van Holland to Amsterdam, and had seen nothing of any interest to entice me to stop. However, in 2020 I took a cruise to South America, which stopped first in Rotterdam to take on fuel and supplies, and there was time to take a shuttle bus into the city centre. What a surprise! The city has been rebuilt over the past 40 years, with no attempt to recreate its historic architecture … instead a range of architects have been employed to erect 'statement pieces' – masterpieces of modern style: Central Station with a V-shaped, steel-clad roof elegantly leaning to one side as if blown in the wind; De Rotterdam skyscraper, seemingly built of separate modular blocks which are slipping away from each other; the Cube Houses, residential cubes tilted on different angles, stuck together only at their corners into a single accommodation block; the Markthal, in the shape of a massive inverted horseshoe covering a food market, yet the 'roof' also encloses homes and offices with windows looking over the market – surely, some homes at the top of the arch must have windows in their floors? Rotterdam is certainly a city which warrants another visit, I think!

SCANDINAVIA & THE BALTIC

SCANDINAVIA

SCANDINAVIA INCLUDES MODERN NORWAY, SWEDEN and Denmark, but can also be considered to include Finland, Iceland and Greenland – all countries with close links to each other historically. In fact, the regions we now call Scandinavia have been switched from one country to another throughout history.

In medieval times: Denmark included its current lands plus part of what is now southern Sweden; Sweden included most of modern Finland; Norway included parts of today's western Sweden and also the 'overseas territories' of Iceland, Greenland, the Faroe Islands, Scottish islands including the Shetlands, Orkneys and Hebrides, and even the Isle of Man. From the 16th century until 1814, Norway and Denmark were united under a single monarch ... in 1814, the Danish/Norwegian union was dissolved, and Norway briefly became part of Sweden (leaving the 'overseas territories' under the control of the Danish monarchy, where Greenland and the Faroes still remain) until popular unrest gave Norway independence, though still sharing the same (Swedish) monarch – only in 1905 did Norway crown its own king. Meanwhile Finland remained part of Sweden until Napoleon gave it to Tsarist Russia ... it gained independence in 1917 when the Tsar was toppled, but sided with Germany in WW2 – as a result some of its eastern lands were given back to Russia as war reparations, and still remain part of Russia today. A totally confusing history, but which has resulted in close relationships between all these nations which continue to exist today.

I never escorted tours to any part of Scandinavia, since my company preferred to send specialist native guides with these tours, but I do have some memories of private visits over the years – and in 1986, after I had started spending several months per year writing copy for my company's next brochure, I was sent on a Scandinavian tour to familiarise myself with the countries I was writing about.

DENMARK

MY FIRST SIGHT OF DENMARK was on a weekend in Copenhagen with my grandmother in 1975 (she was always keen to travel, since she came from a generation prevented by two world wars from going abroad). I remember especially the smartly uniformed soldiers in blue trousers and black busbies, marching outside Copenhagen's elegant royal Amalienborg Palaces, and the ice covering the shallow water around the Little Mermaid statue, remarkably small and perched on a few rocks beside the harbour ... however, my grandmother always described her luscious open sandwich as the highlight of her visit! I returned to Copenhagen on tour in 1986: after a day walking the streets and visiting museums like Rosenborg Palace (a vast brick edifice which was once home to the royal family but now houses their crown jewels), our evening was to be spent in the Tivoli Gardens entertainment park. I was expecting to be bored by hours wandering amid noisy mechanical rides, something like Blackpool's Pleasure Beach. Instead, I found acres of gardens containing open-air theatres, cafes and just an occasional 'ride', all illuminated into a magical fairyland – a delightful place to spend the evening hours. Outside Copenhagen, the landscape seemed unremarkable – miles of flat pastures, kept lushly green by abundant rainfall, studded with pretty villages with cobbled streets and timber-framed brick cottages topped by red tile or thatched roofs. A comfortable, tranquil scene.

Yet that cannot be said of the Faroe Islands, a group of 18 rocky, volcanic islands in the middle of the North Atlantic, located halfway between Scotland and Iceland. It is a self-governing territory, though still part of the kingdom of Denmark. Oddly, it did not join the EU alongside the rest of Denmark and did not adopt the Euro as its currency, so (when I visited in 2012) the Danish mint was still producing Krone coins and notes for use in the Faroe Islands. I was delighted to find that I could conveniently fly to this remote spot from Aberdeen airport (now they are served from Edinburgh) ... though finding accommodation was more difficult. I realised that there was little tourism there, so did not expect to find hotels outside the capital Torshavn, but trawled the internet hoping to find someone offering B&B in the more remote parts of the islands: I found nothing! Eventually I booked into a hotel in Torshavn, renting a car to take day-trips out to explore the main islands, which line up side-by-side in the ocean, divided by precipitous fjords filled with the floating cages of fish farms (one of the Faroes' main industries).

The scenery is a dramatic landscape of windswept, treeless hillsides, grazed by flocks of agile sheep, and awe-inspiring cliffs dotted with the nests of innumerable seabirds. I cruised beneath Vestmanna Cliffs (highest in the Faroes at 600m/ 2000ft), fetchingly dressed in waterproof coat and bright yellow hard-hat (compulsory, in case of rockfall). With almost permanent daylight (it was July), I also had time to drive along many of the narrow roads in the western islands, well-maintained but mostly dead-ends, leading to isolated villages like Tjørnuvik, nestled beneath a ring of towering rocks, or the tiny community of Saksun sitting at the tip of a fjord which cuts deep into the island of Streymoy. The villages seemed quiet and deserted, often with no shop or other amenity, yet I found them enchanting – clusters of wooden homes, often painted black with weatherproof tar and sometimes still with their traditional roofs of grassy turf.

I loved the wildness of the landscape in the Faroes, made more desolate by low cloud and rain showers (the typical weather of the islands) for most of my visit ... but most memorable was the driving. The government clearly spends a lot of money building and maintaining the roads which provide vital communications between the islands – I travelled through well-lit, broad modern tunnels linking the western isles of Vagar (where the airport is located), Streymoy (location of the capital Torshavn) and Esturyoy. I was especially impressed by a splendid tunnel cutting through the mountains to the west coast of Vagar, built in 2006 just to give access to a single tiny village (Gasadalur) – what an expense! However, everything changed when I tried to cross to the more easterly island of Bordoy. In torrential rain, I plunged into two successive undersea tunnels built in the 1960s and 70s – unlit and single-track. I strained to see into the darkness, with the rock walls of the tunnel around me barely visible, peering into the distance to try to spot the headlights of any oncoming traffic in time to pull into one of the rare laybys to allow them to pass. I had intended to continue further east, but with my nerves shattered by these tunnels, and visibility obscured by continuous heavy rainfall, I gave up at the town of Klaksvik, turned tail and gathered my courage to negotiate the twin tunnels again en route back to Torshavn.

NORWAY

NORWAY'S SPECTACULAR LANDSCAPE IS RENOWNED throughout the world, with much of the land covered by towering, snow-capped mountains, sliced by innumerable precipitous inlets of the sea – the fjords, best visited by ship. In 1983, my mother and I took a cruise which started in Bergen, once an important trading port and part of the wealthy Hanseatic League which dominated trade in northern Europe – now the remains of its quays (Bryggen) are protected as a World Heritage Site, a line of brightly coloured facades facing the sea and laced with steep cobbled alleyways. Here we boarded our ship, which (at the time) was still principally a working ferry rather than the small cruise ships which the Hurtigruten line now uses. My mother and I shared the best cabin on board (the only one with a private bathroom) and we ate our meals together with 15 other passengers making the entire journey. Beyond that, our fellow travellers were local people who boarded at various ports along the way, travelling for a few hours before disembarking again further along the coast. We had the run of the ship, so could join them in their snackbar or lounge to chat – most memorable was the Sami lady (one of the nomadic reindeer herders who roam freely across the north of Scandinavia) and her son, both dressed in their colourful traditional costume: blue tunic decorated with contrasting woven strips and a stovepipe bonnet. Our ship was a vital link for many communities, especially in the far north where there were few roads, so at every port we unloaded crates of supplies – food, fuel and household goods. In the tiny village of Kjøllefjord, the cranes even lifted a sparkling new motorbike from the hold, an unusual delivery since the village had no road access and possessed just a mile or so of tarmac alongside the fjord. When we returned southwards again, we stopped in the same village to load a coffin on board, being transported to a larger community for burial – a crew member told us that it contained the remains of the young man who had ordered the motorbike ... he had managed to kill himself, riding his new toy on that short stretch of road.

Our cruise took us in and out of numerous fjords – deep inlets of the sea, reaching into Norway's precipitous coastal mountains. Close to Bergen is Sognefjord, called the 'King of the Fjords' because it is the longest in the country (reaching over 160km/ 100 miles inland) and one of the deepest (over 1000m/ 3000ft deep in most parts). Though the mountains surrounding this fjord are awe-inspiring, in many places they are still studded with patches of pastureland with remote farms clinging to the mountainsides. However one side arm, called the Naeroyfjord, is hemmed in by sheer cliffs which squeeze together so that, in places, they are no more than 250m/ 800ft apart – no space for any agriculture here! Equally impressive is the small Geirangerfjord, its cliffs sparkling with waterfalls. This fjord was one of the highlights of my company's Scandinavian tour, gliding along its waters on a small car-ferry while the tour manager played Grieg's 'Peer Gynt' on the coach audio system, before disembarking to ascend the 10% gradient of the Trollstigen road via eleven hairpins, which had our driver wrestling with his steering to get us around the bends – one reason why the company always used native Norwegian drivers and local, strongly built coaches for this tour.

Sometimes our ship offered excursions inland whilst it continued its journey, and on one occasion we were returning to rejoin our ferry at the port of Kristiansund. We were earlier than expected, so stopped on a headland to watch the ship arrive – it motored busily into the fjord, but did not seem to be slowing as it approached the village. As we watched, it rushed past the quay towards the rows of houses lining the end of the fjord ... the engine had failed! Suddenly there was a flurry of activity at the stern and anchors were thrown out – fortunately, they bit into the seabed in time to stop the ship from crashing into the village. After a time, a large rowing boat appeared, throwing a rope to the crew on deck: once firmly attached, the rowers laboriously heaved on the oars and towed the ship back to the quayside for emergency repairs!

As well as stopping in small villages, our Hurtigruten ferry also took us to some of the larger communities along the Norwegian coast. We stopped in Ålesund, an important fishing port famous for its Art Nouveau architecture – the entire town was rebuilt in this style after a disastrous fire in 1904, with solid stone structures, often painted in bright colours. Further north lies Trondheim, former Viking capital of Norway, transformed into a submarine base by occupying Germans in WW2. We stopped long enough here for a city tour to show us the city's royal Stiftsgåden Palace, entirely built of wood, and the Gothic Nidaros Cathedral, used as the royal coronation church since the 12th century. We were also taken to Ringve Music Museum, a collection of historic musical instruments housed in an 18th century mansion – not normally of interest to me, but I was delighted to find that museum staff played many of the instruments as we progressed from room to room, a musical mosaic which has stuck in my memory.

The scenery became ever more dramatic as we progressed northwards to cross the Arctic Circle. The ship's crew were determined to mark the occasion for those who had never crossed it before, by dressing up as 'King Neptune' and pouring a scoop of iced water down each passenger's neck. Needless to say, my mother and I held back and watched from a distance! We cruised into the Lofoten Islands, where dramatic mountains reared up from tranquil bays and beaches, and villages of tiny wooden homes perched on stilts above the water amid innumerable racks of drying fish. I was struck by the quality of the light in these islands – the scenery bathed in a golden glow, the air so clear that every feature of the landscape stood out crisp and sharp. Before we left the islands, our ship took us into the most dramatic fjord of all, squeezing through an entrance just 100m (300ft) wide (barely wide enough for the ship to pass) into a hidden flooded valley surrounded by vertical cliffs up to 1000m (3000ft) high: Trollfjord.

We stopped in Tromsø, most northerly city in Norway, starting point for many Arctic explorers over the last 200 years. Its centre is filled with attractive wooden houses from the 18th and 19th centuries, but the most memorable building is the so-called Arctic Cathedral, constructed from panels of aluminium-coated concrete in 1965. Each panel is linked and divided from the next by a strip of glass, so that light seeps out on the long winter nights to illuminate the building, and in summer (when we visited), sunlight pours into the worship area despite the lack of full-size windows. A glass mosaic wall fills the eastern end of the structure behind the altar, bringing vivid colour to an otherwise bland interior. Still sailing northwards, we called at Hammerfest – proudly claiming the title of 'northernmost town in the world' and centre of the Sami culture ... in summer their reindeer herds commonly wander through the streets, to the distress of local residents! This town was also garrisoned by the German army in WW2, until the threat of advancing Russians caused the Germans to forcibly evacuate the population, before burning the entire town to the ground in 1945.

Finally we reached North Cape – the northernmost part of Europe accessible by vehicle (another nearby headland is actually a little further north, and Norway's Svalbard archipelago is much further north). Here we walked across a flat, windswept plain which falls into the sea in dramatic cliffs, to see the monument and tourist centre visited by thousands each year. Our final destination was the community of Kirkenes, just a few miles from the Russian border. When we visited in 1983, its main tourist attraction was that forbidden border into the USSR – today there are attempts to attract tourists by other means, including fishing in the icy Barents Sea for king crab or staying in an igloo hotel while waiting to see the Northern Lights. The Russian border is now open, and Russians regularly bring goods across to sell in a weekly market. Hopefully the former tensions between Norway and her giant neighbour, have now been relegated into history?

The coastal scenery of Norway is certainly the jewel in the country's crown, as far as I am concerned, but I should also mention a couple of museums in the capital city, Oslo. When I visited in 1986, our guide took us to see the Vigeland Sculpture Park – a large garden studded with modernistic statues created by the artist Gustav Vigeland in the early 20th century. They have been dubbed 'the Weirdest Statues in the World', and I think I probably agree, though perhaps my impressions are influenced by the wet, cold and windy day when we visited them? On the other hand, we also visited the Viking Ship Museum where three amazingly preserved Viking burial ships are displayed. One is almost intact, and I was awed to stand beside it, imagining the courage of Viking seamen as they explored to the boundaries of their world and beyond, in such flimsy-looking craft. It was so elegant, yet seemed so shallow, without a deep keel or high bulwarks – how ever did they keep towering ocean waves from swamping them?

ICELAND

SHOULD I BE INCLUDING ICELAND in a book about Europe? Geographically, probably not ... but politically, definitely yes! The island was first settled in the 9th century by Norwegian Vikings, and the population today is mostly descended from settlers coming from Norway and also from former Viking communities in Ireland and Scotland – their language is still recognisable as a form of Old Norse. At first, Iceland was governed as an independent commonwealth, under the leadership of the Althing – one of the oldest parliaments in the world. It accepted direct rule from Norway in the 13th century, was absorbed into the Scandinavian union in the 14th century and remained under Danish rule when the union broke up in the 16th century – but it was so remote that, whoever was nominally in charge, the local Althing parliament continued to have actual control. Full independence arrived in 1918, and in 1944 Iceland became a republic. The land is remote enough that they do not have a standing army to defend themselves, just some armed coastguards who mainly watch over the rich fishing grounds which still provide 75% of the country's wealth. I only visited a tiny part of the country during a short visit in 2000, staying in the capital Reykjavik and making excursions to destinations within a day's drive of the city – however, even such a flying visit was enough to give me an impression of the landscape. Much of it is bare rock, with 11% covered by glaciers. Only 20% is even suitable for raising livestock (traditionally sheep), and crops (mainly roots like turnips and potatoes) can be grown on only 1% of the land.

Iceland is geologically very active, sitting on top of a 'hotspot' between continental plates – there are frequent volcanic eruptions, including the volcano which (in 2010) spewed so much ash into the atmosphere that air travel was disrupted throughout Europe. However, Icelanders are experts in using their volcanoes – 27% of their power is generated from geothermal sources, with most of their remaining energy needs met by hydro-electricity generated by their many waterfalls. One of my excursions whilst in Iceland, took me to the Blue Lagoon – a vast outdoor swimming pool which uses the geothermally heated water from a power plant next door. Just the sight of the Lagoon was weirdly exotic, its clouds of steam visible for miles around. Once

I had checked in, changed into swimming gear and taken a compulsory pre-swim shower, I padded across wooden boards and a gritty, black sand 'beach' to enter the water: what bliss! It was a chilly, damp day (typical of Iceland) but the water was soothingly warm, with much hotter spots scattered randomly across the pool as I swam gently to and fro.

On another day, I took the classic Golden Circle coach tour, swinging in a wide circle around Reykjavik's hinterland. We stopped first at the immense 30m (100ft) high Gullfoss waterfall, an awe-inspiring maelstrom of foaming white water crashing over a series of rocky ledges with a deafening roar. Next was the Geysir geothermal area, where the Strokkur geyser was shooting a superheated jet of water into the air every few minutes – I was caught unawares when an apparently tranquil pool of water suddenly exploded before my eyes! The Kerid volcanic crater was a reminder of just how dramatically the land can be shaped by volcanic activity – a massive hole in the ground 50m (170ft) deep, now containing a deep blue lake instead of the lava which would have filled it 3000 years ago. I have seen similar geological wonders elsewhere in the world – but totally unique to Iceland was Thingvellir Park, preserved as a national monument because Iceland's ancient Parliament met here in the open-air for over 850 years (they now meet in a building in Reykjavik), but fascinating to me because of the geology. Here the mid-Atlantic Ridge rises above the sea, following the line where the North American and Eurasian tectonic plates meet – literally the point where the western half of the world and the eastern half meet. The surface of the ground is littered with cracks formed as the two plates move apart at a steady speed of approximately 1cm per year, and I was awed to stand beside the deepest of the cracks – the Almannagjá, nearly 120m (400ft) deep. Where else in the world can you watch the geology of 'continental drift' in action?

The land around Reyjavik is different in appearance, with some pastureland for cattle and especially acres of glasshouses, heated by geothermal steam, where the fruit and vegetables for the entire country are produced. Iceland is the most sparsely populated country in Europe, with Reykjavik as its only large community – two thirds of the population live in and around the city. Yet, as I write this, a volcano dormant for 800 years has erupted just 40km (25 miles) from the capital after two weeks when 34,000 small earthquakes shook the area. The reaction of the local population? They did not flee or panic, but simply took a Sunday afternoon hike to view the spectacle!

Reykjavik is a sprawling, airy place with quiet, spotlessly clean streets. In the centre are low-rise apartment blocks, but most of the population seems to prefer individual houses and gardens in the suburbs. Much of the architecture is modern, including the gleaming glass dome of the Perlan exhibition centre, and especially the soaring steeple of Hallgrimskirkja which dominates the skyline from every part of the city. The church itself is an austere Gothic-style structure, but its facade is astounding – a pointed tower soaring skywards, supported by wide-spread wings: some describe it as resembling an angel embracing the city, though to me it looked like a space-rocket awaiting blast-off. During my September visit, I managed to sneak inside Arbaer Open Air Museum, where a small number of historic buildings, rescued from Reykjavik's transformation into a modern city, have been erected on the site of an abandoned farm – sadly, so late in the season, none of the furnished houses were open and there were no costumed guides to watch working at traditional crafts. However, I still enjoyed a glimpse into Iceland's history, with wooden cottages roofed with turf, squatting low to the ground to escape the harsh climate.

When I visited, the city seemed quiet, reserved and very chilly ... and so expensive! I had hoped to sample some of their traditional food whilst I was there, especially the fish, which is the country's main product, but every restaurant I looked at was priced outside my budget ... to my shame, I found myself eating almost every meal at a local McDonalds (though even that was over twice the price I would have paid at home). I did not find Iceland classically beautiful, but its landscapes are fascinating, awe-inspiring, and sometimes just weird! I look forward to a chance to see more of the countryside in different parts of the island ... when Covid finally releases us again for travel.

SWEDEN

I HAVE TO ADMIT THAT I have few memories of my 1986 visit to this country – but it would be hard to forget Stockholm's City Hall: from outside, an unremarkable, stark, angular brick building with a tall tower, but memorable for its ornately decorated interior, especially the Golden Hall, used for a grand ball after the annual award of Nobel Prizes. A jaw-dropping moment as I slid over the polished marble floor into a vast chamber, decorated floor to ceiling with coloured glass mosaic images set against a gleaming background of gold leaf. Stockholm sits on 14 islands, so there are channels of water throughout the city, but beyond the urban area lies an archipelago of 30,000 rocky and forested islands dotted with tiny communities and hidden holiday homes belonging to the citizens of Stockholm. For me, the highlight of our visit was a peaceful afternoon cruise among some of those islands, spotting traditional houses of red or white planking, isolated sandy beaches and busy yacht harbours.

I also spent a week skiing in the Swedish resort of Åre, located close to the Norwegian border and just 300km (200 mi) south of the Arctic Circle. Predictably, it was the coldest skiing I have ever experienced! There were limited daylight hours at that time of year, so the principal slopes were floodlit to allow skiing in the dark hours of the afternoon and evening. However, as night fell, the snow froze to solid ice (not ideal for skiers like myself, of middling ability) and the sound of sharp ski edges scraping their way down icy slopes was enough to send me scuttling back to the warmth and comfort of my hotel's log fires! I was in the resort at Christmas time, so the hotel had arranged for Santa to visit us – though in Sweden, he is different from our jolly, red-suited old man. He is not even called Santa, but instead is a rather grumpy gnome called Jultomte, dressed in a tunic of heavy linen sacking ... but he did have presents for the children staying in the hotel, at least.

FINLAND

THIS IS A LARGE, SPARSELY populated country of thick forests studded with innumerable lakes ... which I would love to explore, but have not yet reached. However, in the 1990s I did spend a few days in the capital city Helsinki and loved it! There were a few notable examples of architecture, especially the twin cathedrals perched on adjacent hilltops – the rather cumbersome, red-brick Orthodox Uspenski cathedral and white-painted, neo-classical Lutheran cathedral with its tall green dome: both built after Helsinki became capital of Finland in 1812. In complete contrast was the Temppeliaukio church, carved in 1969 directly into solid rock – its bare stone walls provide excellent acoustics and the whole building is lit only by skylights surrounding a central copper dome. However, I was most impressed by the parks and gardens, natural forests and even sandy beaches within the city limits – all packed with Finns enjoying an outdoor summer lifestyle, before the days shortened and weather deteriorated into winter. Even the streets were crowded with people strolling, sitting in outdoor cafes or watching buskers and street entertainers who popped up everywhere – including a girl who had trained her cats to climb a long pole to reach a cushion perched high above (how do you train a cat?).

In one of the parks, I admired the Sibelius Monument, constructed of 600 hollow steel pipes, welded together supposedly in the form of ocean waves – though to me, they looked more like a set of organ pipes. Most enchanting of all was the forested island of Seurasaari, where historic buildings have been transplanted from all over the country into an open-air museum scattered widely among the trees. Most of these traditional buildings are constructed of wood (Finland has abundant supplies of timber), with log farmhouses and mills, and even a timber church entirely fitted out in wood – including a wooden chandelier. As I explored the museum, I was often accompanied by red squirrels, virtually tame because of frequent feeding by the visitors – such a rarity in Britain! Walking back along the shoreline to the heart of the city, I was fascinated to watch people taking the opportunity of warm summer weather, to wash their rugs and carpets on a public waterside terrace, apparently specially built for the purpose with lines of tables where the rugs could be scrubbed, and mangles to wring out the water before they were draped across racks and railings to dry in the sun.

ESTONIA

WHILST I WAS IN HELSINKI, I took the opportunity to travel to Tallinn, capital of Estonia – located just 80km (50 miles) away across the Gulf of Finland, part of the Baltic Sea. Though Estonia is not part of Scandinavia, its history is closely tied to the other countries bordering the Baltic Sea. For centuries, it was ruled by Danes and Swedes, as well as Germans, Poles or Russians ... in fact it only developed as a distinct nation in the middle of the 19th century, finally gaining independence from Russia in 1920. However, it was occupied by Germany during WW2, 'liberated' by Russia in 1944 and immediately absorbed into the Soviet Union. There had always been a strong tradition of singing in this region, and the Estonian Song Festival, celebrating folk culture, started already in 1869 and continued every 5 years throughout Soviet times. When the Soviet Union began to weaken in the 1980s, Estonia (together with the other Baltic Republics) began a Singing Revolution. Thousands of people gathered repeatedly and spontaneously to sing traditional folk songs – in the summer of 1989, 2 million people formed a human chain stretching for almost 670km (420 miles) from Tallinn through neighbouring Latvia to Vilnius in Lithuania, singing their national songs. Finally in 1991, all three Baltic Republics regained their independence from the Soviet Union, immediately establishing political friendships with the Scandinavian nations as a way of demonstrating their desire to orient themselves westwards towards Europe.

My ferry to Estonia belonged to the local Silja Line and I could not help reflecting that in 1994, just a couple of years before my visit, it was one of their ferries which had sunk at sea in one of the worst maritime disasters of modern times. The 'Estonia', sailing from Tallinn to Stockholm in stormy seas, lost its bow doors to a massive wave in the middle of the night – most of the passengers were asleep in cabins below decks and could not escape in the half hour before the ship sank. Over 850 died, including one of my company's Scandinavian tour managers – I saw his name on the memorial in Tallinn, during my visit.

Tallinn was well worth the visit – one of the best-preserved medieval cities in Europe. I spent a few days exploring the historic city centre … plodding up the cobbled streets to Cathedral Hill, once the home of Estonia's aristocracy, to see the ornate domed Orthodox cathedral and enjoy the view over the red tile roofs, city walls and towers of the Old Town from the battlements of Toompea Castle … sipping coffee amid the beautifully restored merchants' mansions around Town Hall Square, so reminiscent of Amsterdam and Bruges, since all these cities were members of the same Hanseatic trading union in the Middle Ages. When I visited in the late 1990s, there had not yet been time to repair all the neglect of decades under Soviet control and the back streets in the rest of the old town were still run-down, with broken pavements and peeling facades – but it was clear just how special the city would be once it was fully restored. Today it hosts over 4 million visitors a year, both staying in the city and visiting from cruise ships. I also took a local bus out to the Kadriorg district to see the magnificent baroque palace built for the Russian tsar Peter the Great, its restoration just finishing when I visited, with fledgling formal gardens newly created around it. A longer bus ride brought me to the Estonian Open-Air Museum – similar to Helsinki's, but even more widely spread out in a vast forest beside the seashore. An entire 18th century fishing village has been recreated here, alongside some historic buildings brought in from other parts of Estonia – 12 farms, windmills, a wooden church and a schoolhouse made of logs, and even a fire station with a red-painted tower poking above the trees. Most of the houses are thatched and fully furnished with hand-painted coffers and hand-stitched quilts ... and I loved the home-made kennel hollowed out of a log, from which a toy dog peered mysteriously!

RUSSIA

THIS VAST LAND IS MOSTLY in Asia, and even its European part (west of the Ural Mountains) has a distinctive character and history which I have not yet explored. However in 2017, wanting to travel somewhere for a short break in mid-summer, I made a spur-of-the-moment decision to visit St Petersburg (called Leningrad during Soviet times, but restored to its original name after the collapse of the Soviet Union). I decided that I needed 4 days to really explore the city ... though later realised that I could have travelled visa-free if I had stayed for 3 nights or less. As it was, I had to go through all the fuss (and expense) of getting a visa – but was glad I had decided to spend the extra day, since there is so much to see in St Petersburg.

By European standards, this is a new city, founded only in 1703 by the Russian tsar Peter the Great. He was determined to provide his country with an ice-free port from which he could trade with Europe, so he attacked a small Swedish town and fortress on the shores of the Baltic Sea – causing an enmity with Sweden which lasted for several generations. It was not the ideal place to build a city, since it was the delta of the River Neva, a marshy morass of islands and tributary rivers. Peasants were forcibly brought in from all over Russia, together with Swedish prisoners of war, to build the city – tens of thousands died in the process. However, within 10 years they had tamed the marshes into a series of canals and riverbeds which still crisscross the city, and constructed innumerable palaces and churches laid out in a formal plan – by 1713 it was declared the capital of the Russian empire and residence of the tsar and his aristocracy. The glorious architecture survived the centuries, though the buildings were seriously damaged in WW2, when the city was ringed by German forces and besieged for 2½ years. The only route by which food could reach the population was across a huge lake between the city and Finland, but it was only passable in winter when it froze … almost a million citizens died, most of starvation. After the collapse of the Soviet Union in 1991, the city once again needed food aid, but it came back to life in the early 21st century.

I was amazed to see photographs of the condition of the city after WW2, with many buildings reduced only to shells, but already during the Soviet era, many were restored and by the time I visited, the architecture was once again dazzling. At the heart of the city, on an island in the River Neva, lies the St Peter and Paul fortress, still fortified by strong walls with barrack buildings inside, but at its heart is the St Peter and Paul Church with its needle-sharp golden spire and interior painted in a colourful mixture of green, pink and gold leaf. This church is the burial vault of Russian emperors including Peter the Great, lying in a sombre marble tomb … and I was surprised to see a side chapel with the tombs of the last tsar of Russia (Nicholas II) and his family, exhumed in 1998 from the forest where they were executed, and reburied here with pomp and circumstance. Many of the most beautiful buildings in the city are in ornate baroque style, like the Winter Palace and Smolny Convent – an elegant group of buildings delicately coloured in blue and white. From a later era, there are neo-classical buildings, including the massive semi-circular colonnades of Kazan Cathedral and sparkling golden dome of St Isaac Cathedral. However, the most amazing building in the city centre is certainly the Church of the Saviour 'on Spilled Blood' – built at the place where tsar Alexander II was assassinated. The outside is a cluster of multi-coloured domes and elaborately decorated facades … inside, the walls and ceiling are completely covered in intricate blue and gold mosaics, and a heavily jewelled shrine sits at the exact spot where the assassination took place.

This church, looking like something from Arabian Nights (though actually modelled on traditional medieval Russian architecture), attracted every shred of my attention as I walked along the canal towards it – so much so, that I was totally unaware that I had been targeted by thieves. One of the group attached himself to me, asking me questions and distracting my attention, while his colleagues swiftly opened every zip on my small day-pack and removed its contents … an umbrella, a raincoat and a small purse containing a basic first aid kit and my spare camera batteries. Thank goodness I was experienced enough to be carrying all my money and valuables in a bum-bag hidden beneath my coat! I did not know that anything was happening until I was suddenly surrounded by a crowd of local Russians shouting at me from every angle … what to do? I just backed myself up against a wall and bowed my head, till I began to distinguish a few words of English – 'thief' and 'money'. I looked up to find that several people had picked up my possessions, strewn along the road when the thieves discovered that they were worthless, and were thrusting them at me. Gratefully I took them back, using one of my few words of Russian: 'Spassiba' (thank you) – an umbrella and camera batteries may be worthless to a casual thief, but they were invaluable to me!

One of the main reasons I went to St Petersburg, was to visit its museums. The city offers 221 museums (no, I did not intend to visit them all!) but the star has to be the Hermitage Museum, the 2nd largest art museum in the world. I realised that my feet would not be able to survive seeing everything in one day, so had pre-booked a 2-day ticket – but in fact, I spent an entire (exhausting) day touring the collections, using the second day of my ticket only to finish off one small area I had missed. Just the building itself is worth the ticket, since the collection is housed inside the tsar's own Winter Palace. Often I found myself gazing at the magnificent ceilings, glorious chandeliers or splendid floors, instead of inspecting the exhibits. But what a feast of exhibits! These are the treasures accumulated over centuries by one of the richest monarchs in the world – delicate porcelain, archaelogical artefacts, jewelled dishes, fine sculptures and masterpieces of art by renowned artists like Leonardo and El Greco. Other museums are spread between various aristocratic palaces – I especially enjoyed the collections of painted icons and lacquer boxes in the Russian Museum inside the Mikhailovsky Palace, though it was a shock to continue to the Marble Palace to find controversial modern art displayed amid 18th century stucco walls and floors of inlaid marble.

On my final day I decided to take the hydrofoil along the Neva River, past the modern suburbs and port, to visit the Peterhof Palace, where the tsars spent their summer months. The interior is predictably decorated with stucco picked out in gold, massive chandeliers and heavily embroidered curtains, though there are limited furnishings – this palace was left as little more than a shell after WW2 and has not been fully re-furnished. However the exterior has been completely restored, surrounded by extensive formal gardens with majestic cascades of fountains. In some ways, I preferred the simpler style of the Menshikov Palace beside the River Neva, Peter the Great's first home in the city, before the grander palaces were built. He was passionate about all things Dutch, and decorated this palace with Delft tiles, solid wooden furniture and cosy tiled stoves to heat each room.

I had expected to enjoy the city's palaces and museums, but was not prepared for the vibrancy of everyday life in St Petersburg. I found busking musicians on every corner, including a young man squatting on a pavement playing jazz on an electrified balalaika with an expression of ecstasy on his face, and a rock band complete with guitars and even drums, surrounded by young people bopping to the rhythm. The streets were constantly crowded with people strolling and chatting, many of them young (I had not really expected that in a city renowned for museums and art). I walked past innumerable fine (expensive) restaurants, and visited one for a special birthday treat, where each course was presented by an immaculate waiter who carefully explained the ingredients of each dish. On one evening, I was able to obtain a ticket to the Bolshoi Theatre (no, not the famous one ... that's in Moscow) to see a performance of 'Swan Lake'. In most cities the opera and ballet companies take their holidays in August, so I was delighted to find here that a scratch group of ballet stars from a range of Russian companies had come together to provide performances throughout the usual 'closed' season. I walked home after the performance, totally unthreatened in the night-time streets and surrounded by splendid illuminations on almost every building. I was impressed with St Petersburg!

GERMANY – EAST AND WEST

THIS IS THE EUROPEAN COUNTRY I probably know best, having explored most of its hidden corners over the years, as a tour manager and an individual traveller, and also visiting friends. My earliest friendship began in the 6th form at school when I became the penfriend of a girl in northern Germany – that friendship lasted until 1998, when she was murdered whilst out jogging (I lost contact with her family, so never learned if they had found her killer, but have visited her grave several times). I moved on to study German at university. During the first summer vacation, a fellow student went hitchhiking in Czechoslovakia and met two East German girls who were looking for penfriends: one spoke only German, so I linked up with her, eventually travelling behind the Iron Curtain to visit her on multiple occasions – we are still friends today. As a tour manager, I frequently conducted tours of both western and eastern Germany, and often made individual visits in the off-season to explore lesser-known areas.

The country we know as Germany is actually a relatively new creation. The land was inhabited by various Germanic tribes since ancient times, most resisting the attempts of the Romans to conquer them (this is the time of the wonderfully nicknamed 'Hermann the German') – the Rhine River became one of the boundaries of the Roman empire. In the 16th century, the region was torn apart by religious wars as the Protestant faith (which developed in Germany) spread through the North, leaving the South passionately Catholic – this religious division still largely exists today. For centuries, the land was ruled as multiple separate princedoms and duchies, with two powerful rival kingdoms (Prussia in the north-east and Bavaria in the south-east) gradually extending their influence: there is still a huge difference between these two regions – in people, architecture, language and food. Only in 1871 did Prussia finally manage to weld the entire country into an empire (known as the 2nd Reich) which continued till 1918. In 1933, the Nazis seized power and Hitler became leader of the 3rd Reich. After WW2, the country was divided between the 4 allied powers – the British, French and American sectors quickly became capitalist West Germany (BRD), and the Russian sector became communist East Germany (DDR). Finally in 1990, the two countries were re-united into a parliamentary republic.

My first sight of the country was in 1969, on a school exchange visit with my West German penfriend, who lived in the beautiful northern town of Celle, boasting one of the largest groups of half-timbered houses in the world – the homes of wealthy 16th century merchants, clustered around the elegant palace of the local duke. As a 16-year-old student, I was less impressed by the magnificent architecture than by the strangeness of living in another country, struggling to make myself understood in shops and cafes with my limited German. I joined my penfriend in outings with her friends – swimming alfresco in a nearby lake, and even trying my hand at my friend's hobby, 'voltigieren' or bareback horse-riding (I did not get beyond simply sitting on the horse's back, whilst my friend stood on its back like a circus performer!). I attended the local school, invited by the English teacher to read aloud a passage in English – afterwards, he told the class that 'she does not have a correct English accent', since he wished his students to speak like the Queen, for example saying 'ket' instead of 'cat'! I was made very welcome by my host family, and on several occasions we travelled into the forested Harz Mountains, once stopping to swim in an icy outdoor pool dusted with fallen pine needles ... and to the nearby heathland of the Lüneburger Heide, walking on sandy trails through the heather, devouring fried sausages with mild German mustard. In the 1990s, I was invited by my company to help create a specialist German tour itinerary, and was delighted to be able to include Celle – by then, well organised to receive mass tourism.

As a university student, I was obliged to attend a term at a German university and chose to visit Marburg – the oldest still-operating Protestant university in the world (founded 1527), though it no longer has any religious affiliations: in fact, during my visit, lectures seemed to be regularly cancelled to celebrate innumerable Catholic saints' days. The old town was attractive, with cobbled streets lined with half-timbered or stone mansions built in the 16th and 17th centuries – after this period, its importance declined and there was no money to change or update the historic buildings. It was little damaged in WW2, since the entire town became a hospital for over 20,000 patients – mostly German soldiers. My visit to Marburg (in 1971) presented various challenges. Firstly, there was a UK postal strike which lasted for seven weeks, so that I was unable to arrange any accommodation before I arrived (no convenient internet in those days!). I was still a nervous, inexperienced traveller, disembarking from a 24-hour train journey, tearfully unsure where to go or what to do. What a joy when a German fellow-traveller showed me how to operate the left-luggage lockers, then directed me to the university offices … and even bought a single red rose for me! The university settled me into a large communal house with other overseas students from many countries – we had a wonderful time together, though we did not learn much quality German, since we mingled the grammar and vocabulary of multiple languages to communicate. During my visit, the British pound was devalued quite dramatically – the student grant which was financing my stay in Marburg, was suddenly worth considerably less. I was forced to seek a part-time job – first cleaning for a lecherous gentleman (I quickly left that job) and then cleaning a Woolworth's store: I will not forget the day when I was called upon to unblock a toilet, discovering that someone had pushed an entire large fish, wrapped in newspaper, into the system!

As a reward for passing my first university exams, in 1972 my grandmother took me on a river cruise along the Rhine – my first sight of a part of Germany which I then visited on almost every European tour throughout my career. The most scenic part of the river starts at Köln (Cologne) with its medieval cathedral soaring high above modern shopping streets reconstructed after WW2 bombing (the city was hit by over 260 raids) – it was miraculous that the cathedral survived, when virtually the entire city centre was destroyed. My guests were impressed by the building, though they did not always reach the golden tomb of the Three Magi behind the high altar, since they also had to find themselves some lunch during the short duration of our visit. I was always glad to move off from Köln with a full complement of passengers, since this was one of the places where guests regularly got lost! Since the centre of the city is entirely pedestrianised, I had to lead my group from the coach drop-off point, through the busy railway station and along a shopping street, before climbing the steps to the plinth on which the cathedral stands. Sometimes guests were enticed away from the group by shops or food stalls, before we reached the cathedral ... sometimes they were so fascinated by what they were seeing that they failed to take note of landmarks along the way ... sometimes they managed to wander off into the shopping malls and could not find their way back to the cathedral (how could they miss twin spires reaching up 150m/ 515ft?). For whatever reason, I often found myself wandering around the Domplatz or through the station, desperately seeking guests who had not returned on time to the coach. I was nearly always successful, though on one memorable occasion I had to leave two older ladies behind – I dared not miss the departure time of a river cruise later in the afternoon. Amazingly, these two ladies responded to the challenge and managed to travel to our ultimate night's destination by local train, even arriving before we did – but I learned a lesson: always insisting that guests carried their itinerary of hotel addresses with them, at all times!

From Köln we continued through the quiet little riverside town of Bonn, which for much of my career was incongruously the capital of West Germany (when the country was reunited in 1990, Berlin was restored as the capital), and past Koblenz, where the Moselle River flows into the Rhine beneath the watchful gaze of a mighty fortress. On my earliest tours in the area, we often stayed overnight in Koblenz ... and it was here that I had to make one of the most difficult decisions of my career. Amongst my group was a single man whose main pleasure seemed to be consuming alcohol – he was persistently drunk, causing many problems amongst the other guests, who were beginning to rebel and demand that I did something about him. After much agonised deliberation, I decided to take him to the railway station, giving him detailed instructions and enough money to buy a ticket back to Britain. I was concerned about what my company's reaction would be to 'abandoning' one of my guests, but I also had to consider the success of the tour for all the other guests, so I drafted a letter explaining the situation, and asked all of the rest of the group to sign it. The last I saw of this guest, he was standing (drunkenly swaying) at the entrance to the station – I never heard whether he got home safely, but neither were there any repercussions from my company.

The next 60km (40 mile) stretch of the river is the prettiest, as the Rhine carves itself a steep-sided gorge beneath terraced vineyards and through picturesque villages. Partway along the river, the water is forced into a sharp bend around a tall cliff – the Lorelei Rock:

"Long ago a beautiful maiden lived on this rock, spending her time combing her hair and singing entrancing songs ... so entrancing that often sailors were dazzled by her and ran aground on the dangerous reefs at the foot of the cliff. On one occasion, a prince's son was drawn on to the rocks and drowned; his father was so angry with the Lorelei maiden that he determined to capture and kill her. He sent all his men to climb the cliff towards her ... many were led astray as they climbed, but some made it to the top. As they approached, she turned to the river, crying 'Father Rhine, receive me!', and leapt into the water. She has never been seen again, but ships passing the rock always throw a few coins into the water, to appease her."

The small boats which took us for our sightseeing cruises, were not equipped to handle the difficult currents around the Lorelei Rock and so we disembarked before we passed it. However, cruising with my grandmother in 1972 we sailed the entire length of the German Rhine, and the crew did indeed throw coins into the water as we passed the rock. They also sang a few verses of the Lorelei song (originally a poem by Heine), so throughout my career I also sang my guests a verse of the song as we drove past the Lorelei Rock.

This scenic stretch of the river is overlooked by numerous castles, each with a legend (or sometimes two) attached – whether on board the coach or on board our sightseeing boat, I was fully occupied for several hours in telling the tales, culminating with the most gory of all – the story of the Mouse Tower of Bingen, a small, squat tower sitting on an island in the river:

"Once there was a wicked archbishop living in this area, greedy and selfish. When there was a famine, he decided it was a good opportunity to get rid of the troublesome poor peasants, so he invited them into his barn to fetch

grain, then locked the doors and set it alight. When he heard their screams, he said 'Listen to the mice in my barn!' In legends, you do not get away with things like that – he was punished by being plagued by mice: in his house, on his tables, in his bed. To escape them, he took a boat out to the tower on an island in the river, because he knew that mice cannot swim ... but these mice could swim, and followed his boat. Terrified, he rushed into the tower and slammed the door ... they ate their way through the door. He ran up from floor to floor, locking each door behind him ... they followed him, eating their way through each door in turn. Finally he reached the topmost room; he could run no further; the mice came ... and ate him!"

Continuing south along the path of the Rhine, though no longer following its shores, our tours led us to the historic town of Heidelberg – its university the oldest in Germany (founded in 1386) yet paradoxically now a centre for cutting-edge scientific research. The old town is strung along the river bank beneath high cliffs dominated by a ruined castle, once the home of a prince-elector (one of a group of powerful princes who were responsible for electing their own overlord – the Holy Roman Emperor). The town was devastated in the religious wars of the 17th century, with up to 60% of the population killed and most of their homes destroyed; the castle was also ruined, but the princes began to reconstruct it until it was disastrously struck by lightning – they abandoned it, and the townspeople began to demolish its walls to rebuild their own town. Now both the castle and town are constructed of the same warm red sandstone, which glows impressively in the sunshine. Our tours visited both the castle and the town, and sometimes also stayed overnight in the suburbs – close by a huge American army base: in the morning, as I waited for porters to bring our luggage to the coach for me to check, I often watched troops of soldiers yomping along the roads, chanting their rhythmic marching songs.

Further south again lies the Black Forest (so-called because the thick coniferous forests covering the hills, look black when seen from afar). Only a few roads cut through the hills, following narrow rivers dotted with small sawmills, still powered by the fast-flowing water – mostly flowing west to the Rhine, but several flowing east towards the Danube. A spring which adds water to these eastbound streams at the town of Donaueschingen was officially declared the source of the mighty River Danube – so the river rises in the Black Forest and flows to the Black Sea, and between the two it can rarely be considered Blue! Where the forest retreats a little, there are green pastures dotted with cherry trees and traditional thatched farmhouses, their roofs reaching almost to the ground, so that they look as though they have caps pulled down over their eyes. We often stopped for lunch at pretty Lake Titisee, its waters dark and mysterious as they reflect the forest reaching down to the lakeshore. When I first visited, there was a small village here with a few restaurants and shops, but by the end of my career as a tour manager, the village had been transformed into a tourist hub with massive coach parks; crowds of multi-national tourists filling the roads; restaurants and snack bars to suit every pocket ... and innumerable souvenir shops selling wood carvings and cuckoo clocks. We often drove away with the baggage lockers stuffed with cardboard boxes containing dis-assembled cuckoo clocks – I dared not question how my guests were going to carry them on their homeward journey, when they no longer had access to our convenient storage space.

Forming part of Germany's southern border with Switzerland is Lake Constance (locally called Bodensee), the 3rd largest lake in Europe at 62km (39 miles) long and up to 15km (9 miles) wide. The main road follows the lakeshore with frequent views over to the Swiss Alps across the water, but bypasses some of the most attractive villages, so I was only rarely able to turn aside for my guests to visit them. However, on some tours I had time to drive into the delightful town of Meersburg, allowing my guests to seek their lunch in the network of narrow cobbled alleyways lined with colourful medieval townhouses. When I visited, in the 1980s, the town was still relatively unspoiled by tourism – unlike the island town of Lindau, which we reached by crossing a road and railway bridge, parking unromantically alongside the rail-lines while I directed my guests to continue on foot to the bustling harbour and its outdoor cafes. My most memorable visit to Lindau occurred in July 1990, when we experienced a total solar eclipse, climaxing just as we reached the village. My guests hurried from the coach towards the lake, equipped with their special throwaway sunglasses, as we were engulfed for several minutes in a soft, brownish darkness – one of the weirdest experiences I have had in my life.

Further east lies one of the most picturesque parts of Germany – the huge state of Bavaria (Bayern). I especially love the far south of the state, bordering on Austria, set amongst the foothills of the Alps – a land of gentle mountain pastures and enchanting villages, where the houses are often painted with magnificent murals. I first visited the area in 1971, accompanied by a friend I had made during my stay at Marburg university. We travelled down by coach, then mostly walked from place to place, sleeping in youth hostels or in woods and fields by the road (we had borrowed some military-grade sleeping bags, and it was high summer), until it was time to catch a bus home – unfortunately, we waited on the wrong side of the road and the bus drove past us. We could not wait for the next bus, a day or two later, since we had to return our borrowed equipment, so instead we hitchhiked, requiring just three rides to travel from the mountains, via Munich, back to Marburg – in those days, we did not think twice about the dangers of two young girls hitchhiking, and did not have any difficulties. The only problem I remember, was trying to get our little camping stove to boil up some water for a hot drink on a night when we slept high in the mountains – at altitude, it is virtually impossible for such a small stove to reach the temperature required to boil water! However, next morning came the magical sight of a herd of beautiful alpine cows taking themselves off to milking, all alone. I still have the letter I wrote to my parents describing the scene:

"We started off very early and saw the funniest sight! The cows, all wearing bells, were coming down the road to milking of their own accord – no herder or dog with them. When they got near the farm, a horse grazing outside, came up to play with them a little, before ushering them into the milking shed. He was obviously so pleased to have company, and yet was doing his duty too."

One of the highlights of this visit was a first sight of the castles of Mad King Ludwig – Ludwig II, king of Bavaria 1845-86. Having studied his story over the years, I do not believe he was really mad, but just removed from reality – he was trying to rule during the time when Prussia was becoming ever more dominant, and the complex political labyrinth of rivalries and alliances proved too much for him. He retreated instead into a world of fantasy, beginning to build a series of fairytale palaces throughout his realm.

He quickly used up all his personal wealth and tried to push the Bavarian government to sanction loans from other European royal families – they decided it was necessary to depose him by declaring him insane. The very next day, he and his doctor went out for a lakeside walk and never returned – both bodies were found later that night. To this day, there is controversy over whether he was murdered, committed suicide, or whether it was just a tragic accident.

The first of his fairytale palaces (founded in 1869) was the mountainside fortress of Neuschwanstein, close to an older palace where Ludwig had spent happy days in his youth. It soars out of the trees like a wedding cake with conical turrets (and is supposedly the inspiration for Disney's trademark castle), and its interior is decorated with warm wood panelling and murals depicting traditional Germanic folktales. Many of my tours included a lunch-break in the village at the foot of the mountain, so my guests could enjoy views of the castle high above them. Of course, many were keen to climb up to visit the palace – unfortunately, this visit takes an inordinate amount of time: firstly, there is the long walk uphill to the entry (or a long wait for a horse-drawn cab to carry you up), then the long wait to join one of the escorted tours around the interior (many of which were fully booked in advance by tourists staying longer in the area). Sometimes, my guests would power up the hill so that they could at least see the castle up close – yet its mountainside site is so constrained, that it is impossible to see much of the building when standing beside its walls. I had so many disappointed, and sometimes angry guests, who had hoped this visit would be one of the highlights of their entire European tour ... eventually I used to recommend that they climbed the easier path to the neighbouring, lower castle of Hohenschwangau (Ludwig's childhood home), from which there were some views of Neuschwanstein. It gave them a sense of having achieved something, though in fact, the best view was from the coach park where we dropped them off.

Much more satisfying was the tiny palace of Linderhof, founded in 1878, and the only one of Ludwig's castles which was completed before his death and where he actually lived. It is a gaudy, over-decorated, rococo palace set in splendid formal gardens, but I enjoyed the insight it gave into Ludwig's state of mind. When he lived here, he wanted to be totally alone – needing servants to run the palace, but unwilling to see them. Consequently, the dining room table is actually a 'dumb waiter' which could be lowered into the kitchen for the food to be loaded on to it, then hoisted again back to the dining room where the king waited alone. This tiny palace contains hints of the grandeur of the French Sun-King's palace at Versailles (Louis XIV was one of Ludwig's heroes), including a Hall of Mirrors where hundreds of candles would have reflected in a dazzling display – Ludwig preferred to live by night, and slept most of the day. The last of Ludwig's castles is Herrenchiemsee, located on an island in the middle of the large Lake Chiemsee. It was modelled on Versailles, though intended to be even larger, and cost more than both his other two palaces together, even though it was never finished. I visited only once, while travelling around southern Bavaria by rail pass in 1974, but was not impressed. I could clearly see that Ludwig was running out of money as this palace was built, with obvious economic short-cuts like using gilded brass for lamps instead of real gold.

In the same part of Germany sits the little village of Oberammergau, usually just an impossibly pretty village with chalets adorned with window boxes full of geraniums, their facades painted with magnificent scenes showing alpine mountains and wildlife, or religious scenes. It is a centre of traditional woodcarving, with innumerable shops selling miniature wooden statues of local herdsmen or mountain goats … and again religious icons. The reason for the references to the story of Christ, is that Oberammergau is famous throughout the world for its regular performances of a Passion Play, portraying the story of the days leading up to Christ's death, interspersed with tableaux representing Old Testament predictions of what would take place. It all started in 1634, after an outbreak of the Black Death plague ceased when the villagers made a vow to perform the story of Christ's passion once every 10 years. In 1680, they moved the performance date to years ending in zero, and have presented the play every ten years since – cancelled twice (in 1770 and 1940) but with two extra performances in 1934 and 1984, to celebrate its anniversaries: the 2020 performance was postponed by the Covid pandemic until 2022. It has become a massive tourist attraction, with 5 performances a week for almost 6 months, in a special theatre seating 4900 people (though the total village population is only 5000). In order to manage this vast movement of people in and out of the village, most tourists can only attend the play if they book a package including accommodation (either in Oberammergau or surrounding villages), transport to the theatre (if required) and a meal during the performance. I have escorted guests to the Play over 4 separate seasons (1980, 1984, 1990 and 2000), though I have never seen the performance itself (the nearest I got was standing at the theatre entrance, from where I could hear the final crescendo of music) ... but I have never had any disappointed guests! The villagers still take it very seriously – 2000 actors, musicians and technicians are involved, but all must be villagers, and they start to prepare a year in advance, growing hair and beards to match their parts: as we visited the village in the year before each performance, there was already a sense of excitement and devotion in the air.

I have so many happy memories of this small corner of southern Germany, including the twin towns of Garmisch-Partenkirchen. When I passed through with my guests, the best I could show them was the pair of hillside ski jumps, built for the 1936 Winter Olympics (the same year when the Summer Olympics took place in Berlin, under Hitler's watchful eye). However, during my visit by railpass in 1974, I stayed in the youth hostel here and was recommended to visit the Partnachklamm – I was thrilled to discover a deep gorge, in places 79m (260ft) deep, carved by a mountain torrent through almost 1km (½ mile) of solid rock. I never forgot the awe-inspiring path clinging to the cliffs above the river, and in 2005 I returned to see it again ... and was equally impressed. Fortunately, I have never had to repeat the less pleasant memory I have of this youth hostel: running out of money during my holiday, I resorted to eating the meal of sauerkraut which was the cheapest they could offer. I reasoned that if Germans could eat such vast quantities of pickled cabbage, it must be OK, even though I detested the taste and found it hard to swallow. I should have listened to my stomach! For several days afterwards I was painfully sick, driven out of the hostel by rules forbidding us to remain inside during the day and so lying by the roadside, unable to move ... I have never eaten sauerkraut again!

This whole region of alpine foothills is dotted with picturesque churches topped by exotic 'onion domes', reminders of the period in the 18th century, when the religious wars finally drew to a close, with each prince choosing on behalf of his subjects, whether to become Protestant or remain Catholic. Northern Germany mainly chose to follow the new Protestant faith, while the South remained Catholic: this new style of church (loosely based on the baroque architecture found in Italy, especially in Rome, but adapted to include locally-loved elaborate decoration) came to symbolise that choice, affirming that the congregation was proud to remain Catholic. My tours often visited Ettal Monastery for a taste of this 'rococo' style – my guests briefly silenced in awe as they entered the church to find white and pink-painted walls, sparkling with golden stucco decoration. All around the walls were painted altars encased in ornate gold frames, and the domes above our heads were transformed by fresco images of heaven. Perhaps I would find it hard to worship when surrounded by so many artistic distractions, but these interiors are certainly impressive.

Further east, the border with Austria pushes deeper into the mountains close to the city of Salzburg, reaching down to the small town of Berchtesgaden. It is a pretty town, dominated by the rocky summits of the Watzmann Mountain and other alpine peaks, but sadly, to most of its visitors, it will be forever associated with Hitler and his Nazi followers. Hitler had spent many happy holidays in the region and in 1933 he bought a holiday home in the hills above the town – it became his favourite residence, and he spent a lot of WW2 here. Other high-ranking officials also moved to the area and the Nazi party established a virtual government office here, with barracks for large numbers of soldiers and luxurious villas for Nazi leaders like Göring and Himmler. The settlement was heavily bombed in 1945, then occupied by American troops and used as a recreation centre till it was handed back to local administration in 1995 – though Hitler's house (the Berghof) was deliberately destroyed in 1952. The only structure allowed to remain in its original form was the Kehlsteinhaus (often called the 'Eagle's Nest') perched on the top of the Kehlstein Mountain (1800m/ 6000ft), which was built by the Nazis as a venue for government meetings and is now a restaurant. For most of my career, the tours I escorted were programmed only to visit a tourist community at the foot of the Kehlstein Mountain, where one of the shops displayed a plaster model of the original Nazi settlement – the best I could offer my curious guests was a glimpse of the concrete foundations of some barrack buildings nearby. Of course, they always wanted to see the Eagle's Nest itself, so eventually I was allowed to create a specialist German itinerary which included time for a full visit. Access up the Kehlstein is via a very narrow and exceptionally steep road, forbidden to normal vehicles, so the first challenge was to try to squeeze my entire group of 40 or 50 guests on to the specially built minibuses which negotiate the road. It was impossible to get them all on to one bus, so I had to delegate one of my more capable guests to supervise the second half of the group while I travelled up with the first contingent. The road ends 90m (300ft) below the summit, so visitors continue on foot along a wide marble-lined tunnel to a massive elevator, elaborately decorated with polished brass and Venetian mirrors (all designed to impress the Nazi party's visitors), which finally emerges on the rocky summit of the Kehlstein, where various pathways meander through the rocks, giving spectacular views across the German and Austrian Alps.

On some tours, I was able to show my guests another side to Berchtesgaden, which has been a centre for salt-mining since the 13th century (still operating today), using a system by which water is pumped into the salt seam, dissolving the salt and extracting it in the form of brine, which is then dried out and re-crystallised in nearby 'salt factories'. This system leaves vast underground caverns and lakes, which have become major tourist attractions. We first entered the mine through stone-lined tunnels, sitting astride a wooden beam pulled by a miniature electric engine – already exciting for my guests ... but they did not know what was coming! They were now organised into groups of 3 or 4, and equipped with small leather aprons, strangely worn back-to-front – all in preparation to descend into the mine workings in the traditional way used by miners over the centuries: a wooden chute! Some of my guests were thrilled to see it, but many were nervous – so I tried always to organise them so that there was a courageous person sitting at the front and a fairly courageous person at the back, with the most nervous firmly squeezed between them. Once the group of 3 or 4 were securely sitting inside the chute, they all lifted their feet and they were off, whizzing into the depths with their bottoms protected from the heat of friction by those mysterious leather aprons. It was all over in seconds ... no time for anyone to change their minds ... then the tour calmed down with a peaceful boat ride over one of the lakes and a walk along a spacious tunnel to see the glistening salt seam in the rocks above, before returning to the surface via an ancient, creaking lift. A very popular excursion!

Bavaria's capital, Munich, is not located in the Alps, but definitely looks towards them – at weekends and public holidays, the population streams southwards down the highways, aiming to hike or ski in the mountains. Even within the city, its citizens love to spend time outdoors in large parks (like the English Garden) or shady beer gardens – I spent many evenings in the courtyards of the Hofbräuhaus, teaching my guests how to lift the incredibly heavy glass litre mugs and swaying enthusiastically in time to the music of an 'oompah' band. Munich was badly damaged by bombing in WW2, but many of its most notable landmarks have been rebuilt amongst the modern developments – giving a wide range of architectural styles. The iconic Frauenkirche dates from the late 15th century, though I find it completely out of place here – it is an austere, brick building typical of north Germany, though its towers were finally topped off by incongruous round domes in imitation of the alpine churches of the south. In total contrast is the elegant, 18th century palace at Nymphenburg – though my guests were most fascinated by the semi-circle of smaller villas in front of the palace, supposedly built to house the prince's mistresses! In the Königsplatz, 3 mock-Greek temples face each other across a paved square where Hitler's Brown-shirts paraded in the 1930s. The new Town Hall is in ornate Gothic style with soaring spires and a performing clock with life-size figures of dancers and jousting knights, which perform twice a day – watched by crowds of tourists in the square below.

The 20th century in Munich is represented by the vast Olympic Park, erected on a former airfield where vast mounds of rubble were dumped after WW2 bombings, transformed into a landscaped park for the 1972 Olympics. The various sporting venues are scattered among these grassy hillocks, including 3 stadiums huddled beneath a single magnificent roof of acrylic glass panels, joined into a 'tent' suspended from steel cables: a revolutionary design in its time. I was in Germany (though not in Munich) during those Olympics, and I remember the excitement and pride of the German people in their Games – this was intended to be the moment when the world finally put aside memories of the country's Nazi past and celebrated a bright new future. On every high street, there were shops displaying TV screens on which anyone could watch the competitions as they took place … but towards the end of the Games, those same TV screens revealed the unfolding drama in the Olympic Village when Palestinian terrorists kidnapped and then murdered 11 Israeli athletes. I stood with crowds of local people, watching the screens in horror, some even weeping, as their 'Cheerful Games' (as they had been nicknamed) were overtaken by tragedy, made all the more horrific because, once again, it was Jewish victims who were involved.

Just outside Munich lies the oldest of the Nazi concentration camps, Dachau – built in 1933, originally to house political prisoners. As time progressed, it also filled with people who were considered valueless by the Nazis – Jews, Gypsies and foreign nationals from occupied countries, especially Poles. It was never an extermination camp but intended for forced labour – though the appalling living conditions and harsh punishments meant that 32,000 prisoner deaths were recorded here, and many more thousands of deaths were never documented. Today there is little to see at the memorial – all the original huts were destroyed when liberated by US troops in 1945, and just two have been rebuilt to house museums. However the story it tells, made for a sobering visit whenever I could bring my guests here.

Further north, Bavaria is a very different state – dotted with once-wealthy medieval trading towns which thrived from the 13th century until they were pillaged by the marauding Protestant and Catholic armies which swept back and forth across central Germany during the Thirty Years War in the 17th century. Over the years, I visited many of these architectural jewels – filled with magnificent buildings created by merchants proud to show off their success; preserved into modern times when the trade routes collapsed and there was no money to build anything new. Some have remained wealthy and are still important cities like Augsburg or Regensburg, but there are innumerable smaller towns, some opened up to tourism by the creation of a tourist route called the Romantic Road. Many of our tours spent a night in one of these small towns, Rothenburg ob der Tauber – a network of cobbled streets lined with mansions topped by high roofs (which acted as storage space for the merchants' most precious goods), all gathered within 14th century walls. Though this town had been renowned among German tourists for many decades, when we began regular visits in the 1980s it was still off-the-beaten-track for international tourism. We were able to drive through one of the city gates to reach our picturesque guesthouse in the old town – modern enough to offer en-suite facilities in most rooms, but too historic to have a lift installed. How we admired their porter, a huge, powerful man who single-handedly carried our 50 suitcases up the steep wooden staircases, sweating but unflagging, often clutching 3 or 4 at a time!

The tourist board in Rothenburg had already begun to offer unique sightseeing tours in German each evening with a guide dressed in the traditional garb of a nightwatchman, who in the Middle Ages patrolled the streets watching for criminals or fire. My company discovered that he could also speak English and arranged for him to come to our guesthouse before his German tour, to pick up our guests and give them an atmospheric walk through the town, recounting stories and spicy titbits of information as they walked. It made a wonderful highlight, but as our guests returned to their homes (in Canada, USA, Australia, New Zealand and other English-speaking parts of the world), they managed to spread the word about this hidden gem – by the time I ceased working as a tour manager in 2000, Rothenburg was swarming with tourists and the 'nightwatchman' was giving tours in English and German every night to all-comers. Whenever we could reach the town early enough for guests to explore before dinner, I recommended that they should visit the St Jakob Church to see its magnificent altar – especially noteworthy because of the central scene representing the Last Supper. In the centre, one figure stands out from the others … however it is not the figure of Christ, but of Judas. It was actually carved separately and is removed from the scene each Good Friday, and not returned to the altarpiece until Easter Sunday has passed. A few of my most enthusiastic guests did actually visit the church, but most were waylaid on the way by Rothenburg's massive Christmas shop! I must admit ... it is also a special place, where Christmas reigns throughout the year, with huge displays of traditional German Christmas decorations clustered around a massive sparkling tree or nestled in cosy illuminated grottoes.

I also regularly visited one of the most important of these north Bavarian walled cities, Nürnberg (spelled Nuremberg in English). The city was wealthy and powerful in the Middle Ages, filled with grand merchant homes and impressive churches – sadly, it was heavily bombed in WW2: a single raid in January 1945 destroyed 90% of the old town in one hour and killed 1800 citizens. After the war, the city was rebuilt – remarkably re-creating its historic buildings so effectively that it is hard to tell today, which are entirely new and which incorporate the remains of the original structures. I would escort my groups on a walking tour – holding a duck-headed umbrella high, so that everyone in the group could see me! We started at the highest point of the old city beside the sprawling castle, passing through a narrow gateway in the walls to find ourselves transported back to medieval times amid magnificent 5-storey merchants' mansions. Gradually we would make our way downhill, following cobbled streets to the main square (Hauptmarkt), dominated by the ornate facade of the Frauenkirche, liberally sprinkled with elegant spires, and by a magnificent civic fountain which once provided fresh water to the citizens. The original Schöner Brunnen (the name simply means 'Beautiful Fountain') was protected through the air-raids by being totally enclosed in a wooden crate – now the original is in a museum, but an exact replica soars above its still-flowing waterpipes, decorated with coloured statues and gleaming with golden pinnacles.

Sadly, this beautiful city is again scarred by its associations with Nazi Germany. Hitler chose it to be the location of annual rallies where thousands of his followers gathered to celebrate his ideas – after the 1935 rally, the Nazi-dominated government passed the law which stripped Jews of their German nationality and paved the way for their persecution and eventual genocide. We drove into the city via the vast, concrete-paved roadway (when I visited, it was reduced to an inconsequential carpark) where marching armies of Nazis paraded beneath a small podium where Hitler stood to take their salute. In the more modern part of the city, we also saw the Courthouse where, at the end of the war, the Nuremberg War Trials were held – 20 war criminals in the dock, of whom 6 were jailed for life (including Rudolf Hess who finally died in 1987, as the very last inmate of Spandau prison in Berlin) and 11 were sentenced to death by hanging: actually only 10 were hanged, since Göring managed to commit suicide the night before his execution.

The far north of Germany is completely different from the south – the landscape is flat and windswept, instead of covered with lush green, rolling hills; the towns and villages are built of brick, in the absence of stony mountains; the language is harsher, including words taken from a local dialect similar to Dutch; the people are stricter and more disciplined, less relaxed and fun-loving than the Bavarians. On my very first trip to Germany, on a school exchange in 1969, I was taken to visit my friend's grandmother in the historic port of Stade, near Hamburg. I have some memories of a pretty town of half-timbered brick houses with high roofs, accessed by warehouse doors and hoisting beams – very similar to the houses I later saw in Amsterdam: not surprising, since both cities were part of the same Hanseatic trading union from 13th-17th centuries. However, back in those days, I was less interested in architecture and history, than in learning about life in my friend's family – I have vivid memories of cooking fish (coated in hot vinegar before simmering to create the traditional 'blue carp' which Germans enjoy at Christmas) under the stern gaze of a wizened old lady perched on a stool in the corner of the kitchen!

On the same trip, I was taken into Hamburg – though all I remember from that time, is a visit to Hagenbeck's Zoo: I was taken aback to see animals displayed in semi-realistic panoramas, kept away from visitors by deep and relatively wide moats instead of bars and cages. I had never seen that type of zoo before, though modern zoos now often display their animals this way. As a tour manager, I did not visit Hamburg again, until I began to escort regional tours in the 1990s, and I never grew to love the city. It is the 2nd largest city in Germany, and the 3rd largest port in Europe; till the 19th century it was a free and independent city and is still one of modern Germany's federal states ... but I cannot find it attractive to visit. The architecture has no time for fussy decoration, as in the south – this is a functional city, full of warehouses and offices, with public buildings designed to impress with their dominant size rather than inspire with their artistry. Admittedly, a lot of old Hamburg was lost in WW2 bombing raids, especially one terrible night in 1943, when firebombs destroyed a vast swathe of the port and the old city, killing over 40,000 people. However, I could find no enthusiasm to share with my guests as we toured the city's streets, and was always relieved when we transferred to a sightseeing boat to be shown parts of the huge harbour complex. In the evening, I was on duty again, taking my guests to the infamous Reeperbahn, lined with restaurants, night clubs and theatres, but also with sex shops and brothels. Prostitution is partially legalised in the city (every port will have 'street workers', so perhaps it is best to control their trade rather than drive it underground?), and there is even one street where the girls display themselves behind windows (as in Amsterdam) – but Hamburg has not made a tourist attraction out of this area, and the street is shielded from the sight of passing traffic by wooden screens. At least I could finish our evening tour in the Planten en Blomen Park, where there is a nightly concert accompanied by dancing illuminated fountains – at last, something my guests could enjoy ... so long as there was no rain!

More attractive, in my eyes at least, is the ancient Hanseatic port of Lübeck. It was a very wealthy and important port during the Middle Ages, a founder member of the powerful Hansa League which dominated trade throughout northern Europe, and its merchants filled the city with splendid mansions and warehouses. Once again, the city was heavily bombed in WW2, and a firebombing raid in March 1942 seriously damaged much of the historic town – however it was meticulously restored after the war. Tourists are now able to walk again between the massive, cylindrical towers of the Holstentor gate, through narrow cobbled streets lined with historic houses topped by typical stepped gables, past churches which pierce the skyline with green copper spires. I always bought trays of Lübeck marzipan for my guests, too – the city claims to have invented this confection (though Iran makes the same claim), supposedly during a famine when all that remained in the storehouses were almonds and sugar: still today, the blocks of marzipan produced here are called 'loaves'. Lübeck marzipan was sold throughout West Germany, and when I visited my friend in the former East, I always took some for her: I was so moved when, on one occasion, I mentioned to the shopkeeper that I was taking it into the East, and he immediately refused payment, saying it was a gift to his brothers in the other part of his divided country.

It is now so easy to drive eastwards from Lübeck, but for much of my life, the journey involved crossing into another country (the German Democratic Republic or DDR) and even breaching the Iron Curtain into the much-feared Communist bloc. I was privileged to have an insider's view of life in the DDR, through letters and regular personal visits to my friend there. At first we were just penfriends, writing frequent letters in which she told me about her life as she qualified as a teacher, married and then helped her husband (a farm manager) to build their own home in a small village hidden in the forests on the edge of the Elbe Valley. Her letters were full of stories of her children, her dogs (she bred Airedales) and her garden, bottling vast quantities of vegetables and summer fruits to store in her cellar for use in winter ... and telling me of wild boar which ravaged her garden in winter, crossing from Poland in search of food. Finally, in 1979, we met for the first time: I was escorting a tour which stopped for lunch in Dresden en route from Berlin to Prague, and she arranged to travel there to meet me. I did not know at the time how difficult that was for her – her journey by train took many hours, with frequent changes. However, we got on very well and made plans for me to visit her home next winter. I had to apply for a special visa which allowed me to travel off the tourist routes, though I was only permitted to visit her district (and had to register my arrival with the local police as soon as I arrived). She also had to get permission to host me in her home (viewed with suspicion by the authorities as she was wishing to meet a westerner, especially since her profession as a teacher was considered a sensitive one, with the potential to corrupt the youth of the DDR). However, in the depths of winter at the start of 1980, I finally set off, following the familiar motorway towards Berlin, but this time with prolonged inspections of my documents and my car at the Helmstedt border. It was so cold that my boot lock froze shut – a very suspicious guard clearly believed I had some contraband inside, so I had to drive into one of the inspection sheds until it thawed: how disappointed he was to find nothing inside (I had all my baggage in the interior of the car).

The adventure continued as I turned off the motorway to follow the national road through the towns of Burg and Genthin. There was little other traffic – cars were still difficult to obtain for ordinary people (my friends had waited for years for delivery of a Trabant, a small car with a fibreglass body and lawnmower engine), and travel between districts was not encouraged. Much of the other traffic was military – either East German or, more often, long convoys of Russian vehicles (my friend always referred to the Russians by their official title of 'Die Freunde', 'the friends', without any hint of sarcasm). With so little traffic, there had been only limited clearing of the snow on the roads – only the centre was opened by the passage of military convoys, so I was often pushed off on to the slippery verges (and of course, my British car had no winter tyres). I had an accurate map to follow, but in the towns there were often no signposts – arriving at a junction, I simply had to guess which way to turn. It was a slow and stressful journey, but finally I reached my friend's village and picked my way through relatively deep snow to reach her home. During my stay, more snow fell – when I left, we had to call out the local fire brigade to tow my car back to the main road! Another difficulty I had not anticipated, was in obtaining fuel – the village filling station offered only the two-stroke mixture used by Trabants, so my friend had to take me to the only place in the neighbourhood where I could obtain petrol.

What a warm welcome I received from my friend and her family, however! They were delighted with the 'western' gifts I brought them, and throughout my stay would not permit me to spend a penny of my own money – a problem, since it had been compulsory to exchange a set amount of currency at the border, from West German marks into East German marks. Before I departed I had to use these up (there was no possibility of exchanging them back) and struggled to find any goods in the village shop for which I might find a use – in the end, I bought a couple of metal casseroles and a plastic waste bin (all of which I still have): the customs official at the border as I left the country was amazed to see what 'treasures' I was carrying away from the DDR! My visit included many hours spent chatting with my friend, trying to explain our very different, western way of life. Though many of the houses in her area were able to receive TV programmes from West Germany, the impression they gave was of a life of luxury and abundant possessions. My friend could not really understand that, though our shops are full of luxuries, not all are affordable – in the DDR, there was little to buy in the shops, but whatever was on the shelves was accessible to every citizen. Most people have heard of the infamous Stasi state police in the DDR, but my friend never mentioned them – perhaps living a quiet, law-abiding life in a small rural village, meant she had little experience of them? However, she was very nervous around the local police (the 'Vopos' – Volkspolizei) and extremely worried that my driving style would come to their notice – especially she was concerned that I only slowed at junctions to check for oncoming traffic, instead of actually stopping and applying the handbrake each time, as she had been taught!

I was also taken to visit all the family's numerous relatives in the area, made welcome wherever I went (in fact, they were offended if I did not visit them on every successive trip to the DDR). On the other hand, I was not permitted to meet my friend's neighbours, since they were military personnel – officially I should not even have seen them, which was difficult as we stood outside on New Year's Eve watching them launch signal rockets to herald the new year! However, this first trip was fraught with difficulties for my friend, since the Russians were already beginning to stockpile the provisions needed to service the Moscow Olympics, due to take place the next summer – there was less than usual in the shops, and some of the country's fuel (mostly brown coal) had also been taken off to Russia. This meant that the power stations were operating a reduced schedule, and there were long periods without electricity. Since my friend's water supply was provided by an electric pump, we had to fill the bath whenever there was power, to provide drinking and cooking water for the day. My friend was mortified not to be able to offer me all the facilities she would have liked, but I delighted in sitting by the fire in the lounge with her two small daughters, telling stories about the fairytale figures we could see in the embers. I was adopted as an auntie by these two little girls, privileged to share their growth into adults – and especially to be invited to the wedding of the eldest in 1996, where they still observed the traditional log-sawing ceremony: intended to prove their ability to work as a team in the first challenge of their married life, cutting through a log with a two-handled saw. Over the years I shared other traditions with the family, including the 'Easter tree' when a branch of blossom was hung with carefully blown and beautifully painted eggs.

There was little sightseeing we could undertake during my first visit, partly because I was forbidden to travel outside the district and partly because of the winter road conditions ... but we did visit the nearest town, Havelberg, squeezed on to an island in the River Havel and dominated by its immense brick-built, fortress-like cathedral. We drove there in my car, parking right in the heart of the town (with so little traffic, there were no parking regulations). When we returned to the car, it was surrounded by a crowd of people – they had seen very few western-built cars, and those were all West German, so they had never before seen a vehicle with right-hand drive. As we tried to push our way back to the car, some of the crowd angrily told us to 'wait our turn' – though they melted back when it became clear that I was the owner of this unique vehicle! We also managed a visit to the nearby historic town of Tangermünde, a wealthy merchant trading town in the 15th century, still boasting complete city walls and fortified gateways, as well as a splendid town hall with a soaring Gothic facade and gables, all built during this period. In the 17th century a disastrous fire destroyed much of the town, and it was rebuilt with picturesque half-timbered houses. When I first visited, in 1980, the town was still struggling with the lack of investment typical of communist regimes – the cobbled streets were broken, the sewage system smelly, the plastered walls of the buildings peeling, and everywhere there was the peculiar acrid stench of burning lignite – the principal heating fuel used in the country. However, as I visited my friend every two years until reunification of Germany in 1990, I gradually saw the city coming back to life, taking its place justifiably as an important tourist attraction. Sadly, I was not able to convince my company to include it in our specialist German itinerary (the age-old problem: they had not heard of it, so assumed it was not worth visiting).

As the years progressed, my visits became ever less restricted – I no longer had to register with the local police, and my friend and I were able to travel further afield on sightseeing trips. We explored some of the local villages, like Jerichow with its massive, brick-built basilica church dating from the 12th century; we crossed the Elbe by tiny ferry, hauled across by underwater chains, to Seehausen, another picturesque half-timbered town behind a monumental gateway; we made a long journey into the forested Harz Mountains (at the time divided between West and East Germany) where we hiked some of its paths and saw the stalactite-filled Baumannshöhle cave; we visited the Spreewald, to the southeast of Berlin, a region where the marshy land around the River Spree has been drained over the years into a network of canals, creating innumerable islands where wooden, thatched houses stand. Tourism was only just developing when we took a punt ride through the peaceful waterways, but when I returned to the area after Germany was unified, I found a madhouse of guided punts, individual canoes and rowing boats for hire. We also travelled to the north of Berlin, where Sachsenhausen concentration camp stood, infamous for its medical experimentation – here political prisoners (and anyone else the Nazi regime wanted to be rid of) were used to test drugs intended to enhance the fighting power of German troops, and also to test different ways of killing prisoners with minimum effort: in this camp the gas chambers were invented. My friend was almost overcome by the stories told by the memorial site – since childhood, she had been told that East Germans were not culpable for the atrocities of WW2, since the Nazis persecuted Communists as ferociously as other 'enemies of the state'. By the time we visited, in early 1989, the 'party line' was weakening and my friend, along with other East Germans, was re-learning the history of her country from another viewpoint.

One destination which I was later able to offer to my guests, was the complex of palaces outside Potsdam, built by Prussian kings (who became German emperors) and used by them until 1918. Most delightful of all is

Sanssouci, built by Frederick the Great in the 17th century as an intimate summer palace – it is little more than a large villa, with just 10 rooms decorated in the most enchanting rococo style (like Ludwig's Linderhof in Bavaria). Visiting with my friend before the borders of the DDR opened to mass tourism, I was able to wander through Sanssouci at my leisure – when I later brought guests to Potsdam, it had become impossible to offer them a visit to this palace since it is so small that visitors are strictly rationed, and we could never obtain tickets. It was, however, possible to visit the much-larger New Palace – also created by Frederick the Great, but this time designed to impress his visitors with the power and glory of Prussia, and only used for state occasions. When I first visited, in the late 1980s, there were few tourists here and we were instructed to slip our outdoor shoes inside massive felt slippers, then to 'skate' our way across the polished wooden floors (encouraged not to forget the corners) – a simple way of using visitors to help maintain the palace! As I took more guests to visit Potsdam in the 1990s (after unification), my company decided it was a waste of time to visit the magnificent baroque New Palace, and instead instructed me to take my guests to Cecilienhof, built during WW1 in the form of an English manor house – I was disappointed to find that there was little of interest here, except a single room where Churchill, Truman and Stalin met after WW2 to decide on the shape of post-war Europe.

In 1978, I was already conducting tours into the DDR, though we were strictly limited on what we could see and where we could go. After a long day's driving, we reached Helmstedt, the last community before the Iron Curtain. Here my passengers would wake up from the bored doze they had been in all day – they had come to see the Iron Curtain, and this stretch was probably the most impressive we would see. First of all came the Allied checkpoint (a mere formality), then we passed the DDR's watch-towers and armed guards, barbed wire and concrete vehicle traps, driving along a pothole strewn road, watched all the while by guards with binoculars. We reached the checkpoint itself, parked the coach and waited … Actually, this border was well-organised and rarely took more than 30-45 minutes. A customs official asked us if we had any weapons or transmitters (but never checked), and the passports plus two copies of the visa list were taken away for inspection. Then the passports were returned, the policeman ensured that everyone had one, and a stamped copy of the visa list was returned to me – we were free to enter the DDR. The only access into Berlin was via the Transit Route – a strip of motorway (originally built under Hitler to create work to bring Germany out of the Depression), lined with a thin band of trees which mostly shielded the huge state farms from our view. There was a single service area, halfway to Berlin, where we were allowed to stop, using West German currency for our purchases ... then it was straight on, without deviation, to the Berlin border. The formalities were less complicated here – a quick check of passport photos to ensure that everyone was still the same person who entered the DDR (no East Germans among us) and we could pass on into West Berlin, an enclave of West Germany, entirely surrounded by the DDR.

When Berlin was divided between the four Allied powers after WW2, the French, British and American zones were soon melded together into a city which came to represent a 'jewel of the West' to be envied by citizens of the DDR – no expense was spared to make it shine! Newly-married couples were offered subsidised housing in the city, to preserve its vibrancy, and as an overseas student in Marburg, I was offered an all-expenses-paid trip to West Berlin, accommodated close to the brilliantly illuminated Kurfürstendamm shopping street, and shown a range of splendid modern buildings like the oddly-shaped Congress Hall (nicknamed 'the pregnant oyster') and luridly coloured social-housing blocks of the Märkisches Viertel erected directly beside the infamous Berlin Wall, as well as the Europa Centre shopping complex with an indoor ice-rink at its heart. Unfortunately, my most vivid memory of this 'gift' from the West German government is not the progressive architecture of the city, but civil unrest in its streets – during my stay, there were student riots which were crushed by battalions of armoured police using tear gas: the only time in my life I have been exposed to the agony of gas in my eyes! When I returned to the city after reunification, many of these western 'highlights' had become inconsequential and were no longer part of our official sightseeing tours. However the Memorial Church, in the heart of the western city, remains impressive – the ruined tower of the original church (nicknamed 'the hollow tooth') preserved as a memorial to the wartime bombing of Berlin, alongside a modern church and bell-tower, constructed as a concrete honeycomb inlaid with panels of blue glass – a glorious sight, especially when lit from inside.

The most eagerly anticipated part of Berlin sightseeing, both on my student visit in 1971 and also as a tour manager in the 1980s, was passing through Checkpoint Charlie, the access point to East Berlin for non-Germans, for a half-day tour of the eastern city. We were given a careful inspection by border guards, comparing our passport list with the actual passports and faces of our guests ... on the return journey, the inspection was even more meticulous, and included examinations of coach baggage lockers and even mirrors on wheels, pushed underneath the coach, to ensure we had no 'stowaways'. The Wall itself (erected in just two weeks in August 1961, to stop the loss of precious workers from east to west) was formidable – a concrete barrier, topped by barbed wire and backed by a wide, boobytrapped 'death strip' where every scrap of cover had been removed. Even the few buildings remaining alongside the eastern side of the wall were abandoned and derelict, with entry forbidden on pain of death.

When the city was divided, most of the historic centre fell into the Russian zone, which remained the capital of the DDR. By the 1970s the East German Government had meticulously restored the most impressive structures along Unter den Linden avenue, including the classical facades of the State Opera, Humboldt University and the green dome of the Catholic cathedral, and Brandenburg Gate was equally impressive – though the Wall ran directly alongside, and no-one was allowed to approach it. My guests were always fascinated to see goose-stepping East German soldiers at the Neue Wache memorial to victims of the Nazis, before we were taken to see the modern structures at Alexanderplatz, symbols of the DDR's progressive economy. They were especially proud of the TV Tower, built in the 1960s and still the tallest structure in unified Germany – tall enough to be seen and admired from West Berlin (though there was an unfortunate light effect when the sun hit the globe at its summit – forming a Christian cross to shine over the Communist city below: the Berliners nicknamed it 'the pope's revenge'). However, much of our time in the east of the city was taken up by a trip into the suburbs to visit the massive Soviet memorial at Treptow – still maintained by the new unified German government, but no longer part of a normal Berlin sightseeing tour.

After reunification in 1990, our official tours of Berlin were transformed. Many of the lesser sights in the west (including the 1936 Olympic stadium and Charlottenburg Palace) were ignored, in favour of newly accessible attractions in the east: the elegant Gendarmenmarkt square, totally rebuilt from ruins in the 1990s; Berlin's ponderous cathedral, partially restored over the previous decades, but now completed and re-opened in 2002 … most notable of all was the Pergamon Museum, one of three museums clustered together on an island in the River Spree – home of a magnificent altar taken (or stolen?) from the ancient temple at Pergamon in Turkey and the even more spectacular, tiled Processional Way from Babylon. The small Egyptian museum in western Berlin, with its famous Head of Nefertiti, faded into insignificance alongside these treasures. Though we used city guides for daytime sightseeing, I was entrusted with the night-time tours and found myself continually confused by the changes in the layout of the city after reunification – visiting once every few months, I frequently found myself lost as historic roads, once cut by the Wall, were recreated. There seemed to be a deliberate attempt to erase even the outline of the Wall, removing any roads which had followed its line – it took considerable pressure to persuade the Berliners to retain a few small sections (though now painted with images and slogans of freedom) as a memorial. One of the biggest transformations was in Potsdamer Platz, originally the heart of Berlin but left untouched in its postwar ruins as part of the divided city's No Man's Land throughout the 40 years of the DDR. As the city reunited, the ruins were swiftly cleared and the dramatic modern buildings of the Sony Centre began to rise, culminating when an amazing conical glass roof crowned the atrium at the heart of the buildings in 2000.

Even in the west, there were dramatic changes to the cityscape, most notably the Reichstag building. It was originally erected in the 19th century to house the administration of the Kaiser's empire, but was badly damaged when set alight by the Nazis in 1933 and further damaged in bitter fighting along the River Spree when the Russians attacked in 1945. With Germany divided and West Berlin no longer a capital city, the building was no longer needed – for most of my career as a tour manager, it warranted no more than a drive-past to see the blackened facade topped by a few struts of what had once been a dome. Through the 1990s we still could do no more than drive past, since the building disappeared beneath a forest of scaffolding as it was rebuilt – finally re-opening in 1999 as the seat of the reunified German government. When my friend and I visited in 2005, hoping to climb the ramps inside the new glass dome (which look down over Parliament's debating chamber below), we found huge queues of tourists waiting in line to enter – clearly now one of the city's star attractions!

Visiting the reunified city with my friend in 2005, she told me of the controversy surrounding the Palace of the Republic, a modern construction with distinctive bronze-mirrored windows. It was built in the 1970s to house the parliament of the DDR (along with art galleries, a theatre, restaurants, and even a bowling alley). It was the showpiece of the country, the pride of much of the population ... but it was no longer needed in reunified Germany. When I visited, a debate was raging as to whether it should be repurposed, though that was complicated by the necessity to remove large quantities of asbestos, or whether it should be demolished and replaced by a reconstruction of the historic City Palace which once stood on this site – it was seriously damaged in WW2 and totally demolished in the 1950s. In my friend's eyes, this debate symbolised the essence of reunification – to her, it seemed that the two Germanys were not being blended back together, but rather West Germany was taking over the East. The power stations in the east had always run on dirty brown coal, so they were summarily closed down and power imported from the west; factories in the east operated with outdated machinery and an excessively large labour force, so many were closed and workers transferred to the west; even small things like traffic lights, which in the east had an automatic right-hand filter which meant you could turn right even if the light was red (if the coast was clear), were altered to the western system. My friend, brought up only under Communist government, was proud of some of the achievements of the DDR, one of the most successful countries in the communist bloc (despite having to pay heavy war reparations to the Soviet Union), but she bewailed that everything she had known throughout her life was being stripped away – "it feels as though we are an occupied country", she wrote, soon after reunification, "we are no longer allowed to be an industrialised nation, but are relegated to a purely agricultural economy, allocated the role only of feeding the cities of West Germany." The controversy surrounding the Palace of the Republic reflected her view – in the end, the DDR-era building was demolished in 2008 and replaced by a reconstruction of the City Palace, finally completed in 2020. I have not yet seen it – but what will my thoughts be, when I do so?

These massive changes were also reflected in Dresden, for 600 years the residence of the powerful Elector-Princes (later Kings) of Saxony, who (in the 17th century) created a baroque cityscape studded with outstanding buildings. In the last months of WW2, the city filled with hundreds of thousands of refugees fleeing the advance of Soviet armies, who ended up caught in a bombing raid on the night of 13th February 1945 – it created a fire-storm which swept through the city, generating temperatures of over 1000°C and killing over 25,000 people. On one of my tours, we were given an eye-witness account of the bombing by one of my guests, now a naturalised American citizen, who was a child in Dresden on that night. She remembered being hustled down into the cellars of her home, locked away for many hours, then emerging to find that her house and all the buildings around it, even the street itself, was gone ... replaced by smoking piles of rubble, in places still licked by flames. After the war, the local authorities cleared large areas to reconstruct in functional, 'socialist' style, but left the heart of the city in ruins, awaiting a decision on what to do with the land, restoring only a few buildings to their original condition.

When I first visited Dresden, stopping only for a short lunch break on tours in the 1970s, there was little to show my guests except the Zwinger Palace – a series of palatial exhibition halls with massive windows, clustered around a formal garden. It was originally built in 1709 to house some of the royal treasures, and was reconstructed in the 1950s and 60s to house an art gallery and the royal collection of fine porcelain, protected from wartime damage by evacuation to the countryside. The only other building restored during this time was the Court Church, built in the 18th century for the king's personal use, and restored in 1962 – an ornate structure, adorned with life-size statues and overlooked by a tall tower topped with an 'onion' dome. Though both these buildings were carefully reconstructed, they were little visited and poorly maintained – the filth of inefficient diesel engines in trucks and buses, together with the pollution of heating systems powered by brown coal, had blackened the walls and dulled the colours of the ornate domes. After the reunification of Germany in 1990, suddenly the historic centre of Dresden became a building site of immense proportions. By now, my tours were spending a night in the city, and I was keen that my guests should see it, as it rose like a phoenix from the ashes. The cityscape was different on each successive visit, so while my guests refreshed themselves from their journey, I rushed out to hurry through the building sites to see where I could safely bring my group this time. One of the first highlights I was able to show them was the outer wall of Dresden Castle, covered with thousands of Meissen tiles to form a mural representing the Procession of Princes (the family tree of Saxony's monarchy) – the tiles themselves survived the fire-bombing virtually unscathed, and we were able to walk along the cobbled street alongside the mural, as the rubble began to be cleared. The Castle itself was no more than a few blackened walls, roofless and pierced by gaping holes where windows had been … but on each visit, more had been reconstructed for us to see, with gabled facades and towers topped again with domes and spires: today, restoration is almost complete, and I cannot wait to visit. As the years passed, more rubble was cleared, though I was still occasionally caught out, when a route I had used before was suddenly blocked by new scaffolding. On my last visits as a tour manager, we were finally able to complete a circular walk, culminating with the promenade above the River Elbe.

At the heart of the historic centre lies the Frauenkirche, a church built in the 18th century by the Protestant citizens of the city. It was hit repeatedly by bombs and finally exploded with the heat, leaving just two fragments of walls and a mound of stones. For all of my time as a tour manager, this ruin was left untouched amid all the other reconstruction – intended to remain as a war memorial. As the 1990s progressed, and there was less and less to see of wartime destruction, I was reduced to showing my guests postcards of the ruined city, to emphasise to them what an achievement the reconstruction was … but at the Frauenkirche, they could see the damage for themselves. However, in 1994, the decision was made to restore this church too, financed by massive international fundraising. It was almost complete when I visited in 2005 – what a shock to see the actual church instead of the ruins I had grown accustomed to. I had really no mental image of how it would look, and was stunned to see a squat, square building topped by a massive dome (92m/ 300ft tall) – not at all what I had been expecting! I have still not seen the interior – that will have to wait for my next visit.

Romania - Hay wagon

CENTRAL EUROPE

CZECH REPUBLIC

A SHORT DRIVE FROM DRESDEN lies the forested Erzgebirge (the Ore Mountains, named for the large quantities of minerals, especially silver, once mined there), which forms the border with the current Czech Republic (Czechoslovakia for most of my tour managing years). Though the distance is short in mileage, I dared not delay my tour's departure from Dresden since I knew how long the formalities at this border would take. In the 1980s, there was always a long line of trucks queuing (sometimes for days) to cross this border. We were not obliged to wait behind them, but they filled half the road, so our coach had to drive for miles on the wrong side of the road to pass them – and they did not usually leave any gaps for us to duck into, if we met traffic coming in the opposite direction. I often had to disembark from the coach to negotiate with oncoming traffic and waiting truck drivers, to allow us to squeeze through. When we reached the border of the DDR, there were complex formalities to complete – passport checks and vehicle inspections, as strict as those at Berlin's Checkpoint Charlie (even though we were not leaving the communist bloc). After a minimum of one hour (often more), we could proceed a short distance down the road to the Czech border post ... more passport checks and vehicle inspections. My guests were already equipped with their visas for Czechoslovakia and Hungary (which I had carefully checked on the first night of the tour, spreading their passports all over my bed), but I was obliged to acquire Czech visas for the driver and myself from the Czech Military Mission, whilst the group were sightseeing in West Berlin.

Finally, we could pass through the border controls and seek out our official Čedok state guide, who remained with us throughout our visit. Sometimes handing over to the official guide was a relief – a few of them were helpful and removed many of my bureaucratic burdens. However, more often they were mainly concerned with their own profit – my guests needed to change some money into Czech Krone, and this was an opportunity for the Čedok guide to access some western currency (a valuable commodity in those days, when western luxury goods were available only in foreign currency shops), at whatever exchange rate they cared to give. On one occasion, I had encouraged my guests to pre-purchase their Krone at a convenient exchange office in West Berlin – the Čedok guide was so angry with me that he refused to co-operate for the duration of our visit. Fortunately, both I and my driver were experienced enough to be able to conduct the necessary tours without the help of the guide, who just sat behind us at the front of the coach, glowering for our entire visit. On other occasions, the guide tried to be helpful, but their standard of English was so poor that my guests could not understand what they were saying – that required considerable tact, to prise the microphone from the guide's hands so that I could interpret his instructions and information to my guests. Yet the Čedok guide was compulsory and essential – if only because I was not told in advance, the names of the hotel where we would be staying or the restaurants where we would be eating. On one occasion, driving towards Czechoslovakia from West Germany, we had a serious coach breakdown, requiring me to organise a replacement coach – difficult in a rural village, on a Sunday afternoon. We arrived so late at the border, that our guide had long since departed … taking with her, the address of the hotel where we were to stay. I decided to head for the hotel where we often (though not always) stayed, and fortunately we struck lucky – I do not think the guests even realised that it had been a shot in the dark!

The tours I escorted, visited only the westernmost part of Czechoslovakia – formerly the kingdom of Bohemia. It was an independent kingdom in the $12^{th} - 16^{th}$ centuries, then was absorbed into the Habsburg empire. When that empire collapsed in 1918, Bohemia became part of the new republic of

Czechoslovakia. The republic was absorbed by Nazi Germany in 1938, but restored in 1945, becoming part of the communist bloc in 1948. It had always been a highly industrialised nation, rich in entrepreneurs and idealists – in 1968, this led to a short-lived attempt at political liberalisation, trying to reform the communist bloc without leaving it. The Soviet Union felt threatened by these ideas and sent half a million troops to crush the so-called 'Prague Spring'. When I visited in the 1980s, it seemed as though the Czech people had given up, their dreams shattered. There was none of the pragmatic 'getting on with it' which I felt in the DDR, nor the exuberant flouting of rules I saw in Hungary – just a sense of resignation. In Prague, historic buildings which had started to be restored and renovated, now lay abandoned, still surrounded by scaffolding which gradually rusted solid over the years; in the countryside, cottages were left to crumble, with no attempt to maintain them, or even add a few flowers to window boxes or gardens to beautify them. Eventually, as the governments in the entire communist bloc collapsed in 1989, the Czechs achieved their freedom from communist control by waves of street protests, and in 1993 the artificial union with Slovakia (which had never been very successful) was abandoned and the Czech Republic was born.

Prague is one of the most beautiful cities in Europe, despite the layers of grime and scaffolding which encased it for most of my tour managing career, yet it was also a difficult city to show to my (mainly elderly) guests, since most sightseeing has to be undertaken on foot. We would set off by coach in the morning, driving up to the highest point of the historic city centre at Prague Castle, but my guests would then be walking all day (with a brief respite for lunch) until we rejoined the coach beside the River Vltava late in the afternoon. Prague Castle is really a fortified hilltop containing a wide range of buildings of many different ages and architectural styles – we spent a few hours walking its streets, seeing many different palaces, one now used as the seat of the President. Since independence, this palace has been guarded by soldiers dressed in a uniform created by a designer of film costumes, on the orders of the first President of the Czech Republic (the poet Václav Havel). He was determined to escape from the dour khaki uniforms of communist times, and wanted something inspiring and romantic – the result is a variety of uniforms to match the seasons, varying from thick fur hats and collars in winter, to sky blue outfits for summer, but always with golden belts, elaborate embroidery on epaulettes and caps, and colourful woven tassels. One of the highlights of a visit to Prague Castle today is the ceremony of Changing the Guard, eagerly anticipated by crowds of visitors, though in fact it is only a low-key demonstration of slow and deliberate marching, with long pauses for you to admire these handsome young men in their glorious costumes!

Another notable building within the Castle, is St Vitus Cathedral (burial place of St Wenceslas, better known as Good King Wenceslas), with its high vaulted interior, immense stained glass windows and soaring spires visible throughout the city. On one occasion, I escorted a group of musicians around Europe in the depths of winter. They had arranged to play and sing in multiple special locations (including the Sainte Chapelle in Paris and Vienna's cathedral), and were due to perform in St Vitus Cathedral too. It was a logistical nightmare! We had an extra trailer for the coach, which transported the large instruments (like the cellos and double basses) but were not able to drive anywhere close to the cathedral – my guests were very unhappy to have to carry their instruments through the cobbled streets themselves. I had hoped to see supportive behaviour, with the singers helping the musicians, but this was a particularly difficult group where each person seemed concerned only with their own needs and comfort, and I failed to build any of the 'family' atmosphere which I normally tried to create in my groups. Finally, we struggled into the cathedral and the orchestra set themselves up, whilst the choir sampled the acoustics. Their eventual performance was exquisite (they were very talented), though I also remember the icy chill inside the church – Prague in winter requires lots of warm clothing, even inside this vast Gothic edifice.

From the castle our tours walked on downhill, to cross the river on the ancient Charles Bridge – a medieval stone bridge guarded by towers and lined with over 30 statues of saints. In the 1980s, this was an easy walk ... by the 1990s, the bridge was packed with tourists, picking their way around street vendors and musicians, each trying to extract money from everyone passing by. We hurried onwards into the Old Town Square, surrounded by historic houses and arcades – location of some of the most interesting shops in the city. In the 1980s, this was the only place where my guests could find world-famous Bohemian crystal (most of it went for export, to gain valuable western currency), but by the 1990s there were shops selling every type of souvenir –

enough to entice my guests away from the principal 'sight' of the square: the 15th century Astronomical Clock which gave a performance at 12 noon, with a parade of colourful figures culminating with a cock-crow from an almost invisible, tiny golden cockerel. In the more relaxed atmosphere of 1990s Prague, my guests were free either to watch this performance or to wander off at leisure … under the strict control of the Čedok guide in the 1980s, they were obliged to wait until the last flap of the cockerel's wings, then hustled off to a nearby subterranean restaurant for a lunch of thick stew, stodgy dumplings and sour beer (a traditional meal which could have been a highlight … but was not!).

There was another strand of sightseeing to include – the Jewish Quarter, which the least helpful of the Čedok guides wanted to squeeze in before lunch, regardless of the evident exhaustion of my guests. With post-communist city guides more concerned about the well-being of their clients, it was easier for me to convince them to visit this area as we walked back to the coach at the end of the day. The district marks the site of the medieval Jewish ghetto, now long gone, though there are still 6 synagogues here – most only museums, but the Old-New Synagogue is the oldest still-active synagogue in Europe. Most interesting of all is the Jewish Cemetery, used for 300 years till it closed in the 18th century. The Jews struggled to find enough space, being forbidden to buy any more land as it filled up, so instead they continually added more soil to accommodate new burials, moving the original gravestones higher and higher till the cemetery resembles an uneven spoil heap, held in place only by exterior walls and studded with a forest of gravestones.

When I was teaching tourism in the early 2000s, one of the courses I taught, required the students to plan and operate their own residential trip – on one occasion, they decided to visit Prague. I made sure that they did not miss out on the classic sights of the city, but they also wanted to incorporate some 'fun' activities (though it was up to me, to work out how to find these locations and how to access them). So we ended up at a multi-storey carpark in the suburbs, where an enterprising team of young men had set up a go-kart racing track – much enjoyed by most of the students. On another day, we travelled just outside the city, to experience Prague's bobsleigh track – a gleaming steel chute running for 1km (over ½ mile) down a steep grassy slope. Many students were more nervous about this activity, since the 'bobsleigh' was little more than a skimpy metal tea-tray, with the potential to travel at up to 60km (37 miles) per hour. Most nervously braked all the way down, so never reached anything like that speed, but there were a few collisions when more daring students hurtled down the track until they bumped into the back of another, travelling more slowly. I was glad to get all the students away from this visit without injury! I was less fortunate with Prague's infamous nightlife: despite its obvious cultural and artistic heritage, Prague has somehow become the venue for raucous stag and hen parties in recent years. One of my students decided to slip away from our accommodation (despite my strict instructions to remain safely with the group), and was not home by the time we rose next day. I was naturally very concerned – these 17-18-year-old students were my responsibility, after all! Eventually, just as I was thinking of calling out the police, she lurched home, drunk and sick ... to find herself condemned to spend the rest of the trip sleeping in an annexe off my room, where I could keep an eye on her.

HUNGARY

SOME OF MY TOURS TRAVELLED to Hungary from Vienna, whilst others took the highway from Prague, straight through the Slovak part of the country, to the Hungarian border ... but it was always a much more relaxed border crossing than we had experienced in the DDR or Czechoslovakia. The coach was searched only cursorily (if they even remembered), the passports were checked on the bus itself, and the only delay was the purchase of visas for the driver and myself. Hungary was one of the few Warsaw Pact countries which had no direct borders with the Soviet Union, and perhaps because of that, they seemed to feel less threatened by the looming presence of their giant 'friend'.

Of course, they also had a long history of powerful independence: from the 12th to 15th centuries Hungary was the dominant power in their region, until they were partially occupied by Ottoman Turks in the 16th century. The Turks were replaced by the Austrian Habsburgs in the 18th century – but within 100 years they had become equal partners in the Austro-Hungarian empire, until it collapsed in 1918. After WW1, the borders in eastern Europe were re-drawn and Hungary lost 71% of their former lands, leaving many Hungarian-speaking enclaves in neighbouring countries. They chose to ally themselves with Germany in WW2 and were rewarded by the reinstatement of their former territories, only to lose them all again at the end of the war, when they became a satellite state of the USSR. At first they were oppressed by a very strict regime, but after a national revolt in 1956, the Hungarians managed to create a more relaxed form of communism (nicknamed 'Goulash Communism') with higher living standards and economic reforms, achieving what the Czechs had failed to do: censorship was less strict, church-going was no longer banned, and foreign travel was allowed every three years (though there was a shortage of western currency for these trips, leading to a lively black market – we were constantly accosted in the streets by people offering to exchange our hard currency for thick wads of Forints). The Soviet Union permitted these reforms, since Hungary still had close links with Austria and therefore provided a useful 'bridge' with the capitalist West. In September 1989, the government removed the barbed wire 'Iron Curtain' between Hungary and Austria – allowing other eastern Europeans (especially East Germans) a legal escape route from their own countries to the West. In effect, Hungary precipitated the end of the Warsaw Pact – just two months later, the Berlin Wall fell.

Even travelling towards Budapest in the 1970s and 80s, my guests could sense the difference between Hungary and other eastern European countries – instead of vast State-owned farms, the road was lined with co-operatives, where groups of farmers or villages worked together to produce the crops specified by the government, selling them to the State and sharing the profit amongst themselves. The villages were composed of small cottages (often painted in vibrant 'Habsburg yellow'), each surrounded by fertile personal gardens filled with vegetables, vines and flowers. The towns along the way were full of the usual drab, socialist-style housing blocks, interlaced with huge, insulated pipes carrying hot water from the power plants to heat these blocks (though the insulation was often hanging loose in shreds) – but even here, there were a few interesting monuments with ornate facades and onion domes, dating from the Habsburg era. Budapest was jammed with traffic – everyone seemed to be able to afford a car, though often they were cheap Trabants, and buses and trucks churned out filthy exhaust fumes which blackened the city centre's buildings. I was especially fascinated by the extra-long 'bendy' buses, articulated in the centre so that they could navigate street corners: they drove at top speed down Andrássy Út, Budapest's principal shopping street, with the 10m rear section taking off for a few moments after each crunching pothole (we nicknamed them the 'flying buses').

Our hotels were always located on or close to Andrássy Út, so my guests had plenty of time to absorb the vibrant (if noisy and dirty) atmosphere – though I had to warn them not to be tempted to step out on to the tiny balconies overlooking the street, since none of the hotels was well-maintained and I was always afraid that a balcony would give way beneath their feet. The hotels dated from the 19th century and were suitably grand and spacious, though the plumbing often leaked and wires hung loose from the walls ... but what an experience to take dinner in a vast vaulted dining hall, where gypsy musicians wandered from table to table making their violins sing impossibly high notes, while in the centre of the room another musician played a traditional cimbalom, like a large zither played with cotton-wrapped sticks, often at tremendous speed and with amazing skill. In the evenings, we attended a formal Folklore Evening, with more of this exhilarating gypsy music combined with energetic dances where men whirled and leaped, while ladies glided across the stage, seemingly without moving their feet, carrying pottery jugs on their heads. In Hungary there were no strict government 'minders' to organise every moment of our visit, so there was time in the afternoons for my guests to visit an elegant coffee shop and sample cakes which were the equal of anything Vienna could offer. On one occasion, my city guide (who also became a friend) organised an afternoon at the hairdresser for me, a vast salon where I was passed from section to section – first one assistant washed my hair (accompanied by a delicious head massage), then another set it with rollers, finally a third dried and styled it. The afternoon culminated with hand massage: a real treat!

Having become friends with this city guide, she made every effort to be available whenever I visited the city. I might have lost touch once my allocated tours changed and I ceased to visit Budapest, but she was keen to continue a pen-friendship and so I learned that she had managed to obtain a visa to visit Paris, where she met a handsome Egyptian who swept her off her feet with promises of marriage and an escape from the restrictions of life in communist Hungary. Some years later, I visited her in her new home in

Alexandria – but the dream was already spoiled: once in Egypt, she was expected to behave like a good Muslim wife, remaining in the family home under the domination of her mother-in-law and not permitted to take employment. She ran away, vanishing for some years back into Europe, pursued by her furious husband, then once again contacted me. The last time I saw her, she had remarried and settled into a quiet life in Austria.

City sightseeing in Budapest started with a coach tour around the once separate community of Pest, sprawling along the flat banks of the Danube River (it was only united with hilltop Buda in 1873). We passed many imposing buildings dating from the city's 19th century Golden Age, when it was joint capital of the Habsburg empire, finally arriving in Hero Square where the classical facades of two art galleries enclose a vast space surrounding a column and colonnade where statues of important national heroes stand proudly – including the horseback figures of the 7 Magyar chieftains who are considered the founders of the Hungarian nation. Though the name of the country implies that it originated with Attila the Hun (who marauded right across Europe and the Middle East in the 6th century), in fact it was the Magyars under Prince Árpád, who conquered the region in the 9th century – the Hungarians call themselves Magyars and their country the Magyar State. Behind Hero Square lie the wide green spaces of the City Park, and inside it are the imposing buildings of Szĕchenyi Thermal Baths – enclosing two of the city's 80 geothermal springs. On one occasion, an especially friendly group of ladies among my guests, invited me to join them when they visited this spa during their afternoon at leisure. We first bathed in the deliciously warm outdoor pools (ranging from 23° to 25°C), then settled into one of the massage rooms – pummelled and pounded by a huge lady, then scrubbed with loofahs in a welter of soapsuds. We emerged feeling squeaky clean, reluctant to allow the city's dirty air to pollute our purity!

Sightseeing continued across the Danube, passing the historic Chain Bridge (designed by an Englishman, built by a Scot, funded by a Greek) which was considered an engineering marvel when it opened in 1849. Then came a steep climb uphill to Buda's Castle District – hard enough for modern coaches, but on one occasion we had an ancient substitute coach with no power steering: how the young driver sweated as he hauled on the steering wheel to negotiate the bends! Here we walked amid picturesque, cobbled streets, lined with the elegant mansions of Habsburg-era nobility and with brightly coloured townhouses, as far as the medieval Matthias Church with its dramatic diamond-patterned roof. Finally, we climbed on to the Fisherman's Bastion, once part of a fortification wall but rebuilt in the early 20th century as a viewing terrace, adorned with pointed turrets like a Disney castle. The spectacular view encompasses the whole of Pest, but especially the vast Parliament building (3rd largest of its type in the world). It was created in the 19th century to reflect the glory of the Habsburg empire, but now only part is still used by the government – the rest is available for conferences and tourist visits. Since 2001 it has also been home to the Hungarian crown jewels, including the 12th century Crown of St Stephen, rescued from the Nazis by American troops and held for safety in Fort Knox for much of the Soviet period.

Sadly, none of my tours included further exploration of Hungary – we always headed southwest, either back into Austria or into Yugoslavia (now Croatia). However, there was one last lunch-stop to enjoy, close to the vast inland sea of Lake Balaton, largest lake in Central Europe (77km/ 48 mi long). Sometimes we travelled along the southern shore of the lake, passing resort towns and crowded beaches – the lake is shallow, with an average depth of just 3m (10 feet), and so the water warms up to temperatures of 25°C in summer. Through the 1960s and 70s, it was a destination for subsidised holidays for state workers, and also became popular with visitors from other Eastern European countries, especially East Germans. By the 1980s, West Germans were also allowed to visit, so the region became an unofficial place of reunion for divided German families. More often, we travelled along the northern shore of the lake, through hillsides covered in vineyards producing fine white wines. Often our lunch stop was arranged in a pretty wine tavern, with walls hung with strings of dried, bright red paprika, like bunches of cherries – our guests were invited to break off pieces to add to their goulash soup, but warned not to use too much. On one occasion, a guest broke off a small piece, then another, then another, but it was clearly a dud, as there seemed to be no effect. So he boldly took a whole paprika from the next string … and spent the next half hour gasping and groaning as his soup burned its way down his throat and through his stomach!

ROMANIA

THOUGH I NEVER WORKED IN the easternmost countries of Europe, for many years I had been interested in the folk culture of Romania. In 2010 I finally took a tour into the country, though I should not have waited so long – just three years earlier Romania had joined the European Union, giving them access to innumerable development grants: good news for the Romanians, but the death knell for traditional lifestyles. The country did seem to be trying to preserve highlights of its heritage – but what might Romania's 'national' heritage be? Until the end of WW1, there was no single country named Romania – it was divided into three separate nations by the hook-shaped Carpathian mountain range. The western section (Transylvania) belonged for much of its history to Hungary, then to the Austro-Hungarian empire ... the southern section (Wallachia) was occupied for much of its history by Turks ... the north-eastern section (Moldavia) was often under the domination of Russians – still today, part of Moldavia exists as a separate country (Moldova).

Even as a tourist, I could see distinct differences between the regions. We started in the capital, Bucharest (in Wallachia) – which reminded me strongly of Vienna with wide avenues and massive baroque city palaces (now housing museums and offices). Parts of the city were still full of severe Communist-style architecture (Romania was a socialist republic1947-89) with austere blocks of flats ... and the immense palace which President Ceauçescu built for himself (second largest building in the world), now used as offices and a congress centre. In many places 19th century buildings had been demolished, retaining only their facades to disguise the modern glass and steel structures built up behind them – the newly acquired wealth of the country was clearly evident. We left Bucharest to head directly into the thickly forested Carpathian Mountains, stopping in the foothills to see the pinnacled confection of Peles Castle and smaller Pelisor Palace, both built for the royal family in the late 19th century, seized by the Communist state but returned to the (now deposed) royal family in 2006. We toured the smaller palace, used by Queen Marie as a 'country-style' summer home, full of small intimate rooms with wood-panelled walls – though her favourite room was entirely covered with gold leaf!

Driving through the Carpathians took us into Transylvania, a peaceful landscape where sheep grazed on glorious alpine meadows. After a night in a tranquil hamlet, it was a shock to arrive in the nearby village of Bran, packed with buses and minibuses, wandering hordes of camera-toting tourists, shops selling souvenirs (and blue jeans), restaurants selling pizza and frankfurters – this was clearly the one place in Romania known to the outside world! All the excitement was caused by imposing Bran Castle, built by the city of Braşov in the 14th century to guard (and exact tolls from) a pass through the mountains. In 1920, unable to pay for its maintenance any longer, the city donated the castle to Queen Marie as another summer residence. However it became world-famous when, in the 1960s, clever marketing branded the fortress as 'Dracula's Castle' – hence the crowds of visitors. In fact, it has nothing to do with Dracula, who was a 15th century prince in Wallachia (across the mountains), also known as Vlad the Impaler, because of his vicious treatment of prisoners taken in wars against the Turks. However, the castle's appearance matches descriptions in the book by Bram Stoker, so … as I said, clever marketing!

We continued to the nearby walled city of Braşov, also known as Kronstadt – this whole area of Carpathian foothills was settled by Germans in the 12th century, who only left when offered citizenship in Germany in 1990. The Black Church (so called because the walls were left charred after it was attacked in the 17th century) is a typical North German brick edifice, adorned inside by many brightly coloured carpets donated by wealthy merchants. On the other hand, the Town Square reminded me strongly of towns in south-eastern Austria, with beautifully restored baroque buildings gathered around an imposing 'Habsburg yellow' town hall. Just outside the city walls, a Bavarian-style beer festival was underway, with customers drinking beer from huge 'steins', seated at long tables while a brass band played 'oompah music'. As evening fell, a crowd gathered in the main square for a free concert by the Braşov Symphony Orchestra, playing a variety of Viennese classics accompanied by both professional dancers and children from a local dance school – can you visualise a display of break-dancing to the sound of Beethoven's Fifth Symphony?

After the concert, we boarded a (very bumpy) overnight train north to the Maramures region (on the Ukrainian border) where a breakfast feast was organised for us by a local family: fresh bread, sheep cheese, meatballs, tomatoes and cucumber, all washed down with 'palinka' (schnapps ... for breakfast!). In the nearby village of Sapanta, we finally had a glimpse of traditional rural life, including a communal 'washing machine' – a fast-flowing stream has been partially dammed to create a head of water which, when the sluice is opened, cascades down into a large wooden tub with enough force to pound the dirt from carpets and rugs (it would be much too powerful for more delicate fabrics). In the same village, we visited the renowned Merry Cemetery: since the 1930s, the grave markers have been carved and painted with pictures and epitaphs picking out distinctive character traits of the dead person, as reported by local gossip – including a drunk, a man who was henpecked and a strident woman. The Orthodox faith is clearly important in this region, and every village boasts a traditional wooden church (the Habsburg rulers had only permitted Catholic churches to be built with stone) – the most impressive being the beautiful 18th century church of Bogdan Voda, where every inch of walls and ceiling is covered with vivid paintings.

Next day we rose well before dawn to drive deep into the forests for our first day-trek in the Carpathian Mountains. Our guide worked as a forester when he was not escorting groups, so he was able to give us a first-hand account of this important industry, describing how the forests are harvested on a rotating system, taking all the best trees from one area before replanting and moving on. The trees often grow on such steep slopes that it is not possible to use machinery, so we saw horses being used to pull the trees down into the valley where tractors are hitched to them, dragging the timber down the river valleys until they reach a road or track. Our day in the mountains started with a ride on a privately-owned logging train – there is a network of narrow-gauge lines throughout the forest, many overgrown and unused until their section of forest is due again for harvesting. The loggers travel by rail into their working area at the start of each week, sleeping in a basic caravan or hut through the week, returning home by train for the weekend. We boarded a simple carriage with wooden seats and open, glassless windows, scrambling over a pile of metal hawsers partially blocking the doorway, then chugged off slowly, till a shout to the engine driver stopped the train beside a narrow tributary valley. Here we disembarked, following a wet and muddy logging track steeply uphill through forests redolent with the scent of pine, passing right over the main ridge of the Carpathians to leave Transylvania and enter Moldavia.

Next morning brought another trek, though this time we were able to ascend the ridge using a rickety old chairlift, walking on broad trails amid herds of Alpine cattle (their bells clanging lazily), where hay was drying on racks, and fishermen were casting their lines into the rivers. Eventually we rejoined our coach to drive into the town of Campulung Moldovenesc, which offered me a multi-lingual experience – using German in one shop and Italian in another. Before my visit, I had expected to hear a Slavic language in Romania (as in most of Eastern Europe), but I quickly learned that (after the Roman empire defeated the original Dacian people back in the 2nd century AD) large numbers of Roman veteran soldiers had settled here, establishing Latin as the country's language. At some point around the 5th century, that Latin transmuted into Romanian, a language with many similarities to modern Italian. I suppose I should have guessed at this history, since the country actually bears the name of the Romans!

Villages in Moldavia have a very different appearance from those to the west of the mountains, with houses mostly built of stone or brick, instead of wood, and seeming wealthier and more comfortable. Almost every house has a well in the front garden, often enclosed in an elaborate kiosk and accessed by a huge wheel to pull up the bucket – our guide told us that this water is still considered best for consumption, though 90% of the country is now connected to the mains. The churches are very different too – built of stone, enclosed within strong walled compounds which also house a monastery or nunnery … with painted murals both inside and out. In the 15th century, Moldavia was ruled over by the powerful king Stephen the Great, who gave refuge to floods of artists (seeking the nearest Orthodox haven) when Istanbul fell to the Turks. He fought many battles against the Turks, and after each victory he founded a church, many of them fabulously decorated … his successors over the next century followed his lead. Our first sight of these churches was at Moldovita Monastery (built 1532), where the painted exterior of the church presents such a riot of colourful scenes and images, that I hardly knew where to look first. We continued to the massive, fortified walls of Sucevita Monastery (1583), where both exterior and interior walls are packed with images – originally used as teaching aids by the priests.

We had one more day-trek to complete, this time walking from one church to another: from Sucevita to Putna. We scrambled up a slope through the deep silence of thick forest, punctuated only by the whistles of invisible birds and the distant buzz of loggers' chainsaws, then descended to a broad river valley ... to find it devasted by recent major floods. The riverbed was clogged with stony rubble and crushed trees, and (lower down) we traversed villages where newer houses had been rendered uninhabitable with their foundations partly washed away (the older houses had been sensibly built well back from the river). The route was not as steep as our first trek, though the path was even more muddy – often churned to destruction by the passage of logging tractors. However, the advantage of mud is that animal tracks are nicely preserved – including a bear's front paw, then a huge rear paw (almost like a human foot). Putna Monastery was a disappointment for me – it is vaunted as the oldest of Romania's painted churches, founded by Stephen the Great himself (who is buried there), but the original building was rebuilt in the 17th century with no exterior paintings, and large interior paintings representing just patrons and saints, lacking the tiny blocks of images telling individual stories, which had fascinated me in Moldovita and Sucevita.

Now our goal was the Danube delta. We travelled through fertile farmland in the valley of the Siret River, then continued to Tulcea to board our floating 'ponton' hotel for the last days of the tour, floating through the complex channels of the Danube delta. I had envisaged that a ponton would be a basic barge-like boat, but in fact they are comfortable river cruisers without engines – so we were pulled by a small tugboat as we slid out into the maze of channels which make up the Delta. We spent two days being towed peacefully around the channels, watching abundant birdlife among the reedbeds, swamps and tangled willow thickets; dozing in the sun ... and slapping at mosquitoes!. We stopped briefly to visit a village, hidden in the depths of the delta and accessible only by boat – one of several settlements established by Russians who fled persecution under the Tsars to hide away in these remote marshes. We also made a few forays in the ponton's motor-launches, travelling along shallower channels into vegetation-choked lakes in search of birds. What a delightful way to finish our visit to Romania!

POLAND

I NEVER ESCORTED TOURS INTO Poland, and only visited once – in the 1990s, on a training tour specially organised by my company for its tour managers. However, I have a few vivid memories of that trip, learning for the first time about the tragic history of Poland. This was a wealthy and influential country in the 16th and 17th centuries, but then began to be dominated by its powerful neighbours: Russia, Prussia and Austria. They claimed more and more of Poland's territories, until by 1795 there was nothing left – Poland ceased to exist, and the Polish language and culture began to fade, except in the southern city of Krakow. After WW1, the Allies chose to recreate the country, but in 1939, both Russia and Germany invaded from opposite directions, within a few weeks of each other, and began genocides of Polish people – 6 million Poles (half of them Jews) were killed; large numbers of younger Poles fled, many joining the western Allies fighting in WW2. After the war, Russia kept the eastern part of Poland, whilst Germany had to cede a slice of its territory to become the western part – millions of Poles were forced to migrate hundreds of miles from one end of the newly restructured state to the other. Russia then enforced its dominance in the entire country, crushing anti-communist rebellions until the independent trade union Solidarity was founded in 1980, gradually transforming into a political power which weakened the communist government till it collapsed in 1989. We visited the country a few years later, finding a nation enthusiastically embracing the principles of capitalism – in several restaurants, I remember the waiters surreptitiously opening their jackets to display jars of caviar which they wished to sell us, before serving our food!

In the capital city, Warsaw, nothing remains of the original city (which was bombed and then razed to the ground by retreating Nazis) but I was amazed to see the way in which the historic Market Square was recreated (in the 1950s) – it looks just as it did in the 17th century, surrounded by mansions once inhabited by wealthy merchant families. The skills developed by Polish craftsmen as they rebuilt Warsaw, made them much sought-after as the rest of Europe began to restore their war-damaged cities. We were also proudly shown the 'jewel' of the city's socialist architecture – the 237m (780ft) tall concrete skyscraper of the Palace of Culture ... but I am afraid, it did not impress me. I was moved far more by the memorial to the Warsaw Uprising in 1944 – a cluster of free-standing, life-sized, bronze statues, portrayed emerging from ruined buildings with guns in hand, or slipping away into the ground, using the sewer system to outflank the German soldiers. Sadly, only a small part of historic Warsaw was reconstructed – most of the ruins were replaced by functional, cheap, prefabricated housing blocks.

It is a very different story in Krakow, which escaped bombing in WW2 and therefore has preserved many of its historic buildings from the time when it was capital of Poland – the streets are lined with city palaces reminiscent of Vienna, with large arched doorways at ground level (now usually filled by shops) which were once the entrances to stables, then servants' accommodation on the first floor (where the smell of the stables was strong), and the family's chambers, with elaborately decorated windows, on the second floor. Especially memorable is the Market Square, surrounded by the elegant facades of mansions built in the 13th century, now painted in a variety of soft colours. In the heart of the square stands the Cloth Hall, with its long, arcaded porch – once the merchants' trade hall, now filled with tourist shops. Also in the square is St Mary's Basilica, notable for its odd mis-matched towers: as we visited it, we were serenaded by a bugler playing from a window in one of the towers, though his performance was strangely cut off in the middle of one of the notes – legend says that the tradition dates from the 13th century, when a bugler sounding an alarm as enemy troops approached, was killed by an arrow to his throat whilst in the middle of his call.

In the outskirts of Krakow lie the Wieliczka Salt Mines – probably the most impressive underground caverns I have ever visited. Hundreds of steps lead down through passages where the walls gleam with seams of salt, and the air is cool and surprisingly salty on the lips. The walkways suddenly emerge on a balcony overlooking a vast chamber which has been transformed into St Kinga's Chapel, adorned with murals cut directly into the rock-salt walls, portraying religious scenes – including a copy of Leonardo's 'Last Supper'. Intricate statues of various saints stand in niches carved into the sides of the cavern, including one of Pope John Paul II (one of the most memorable popes of recent times, in office from 1978 to 2005), who came from Poland. The whole scene is lit by massive, glistening chandeliers created from pieces of pure rock salt, suspended high above visitors' heads. We were told that these sculptures were created by miners, choosing to spend their relaxation time deep in the mine instead of struggling back to the surface, and to pass that time by carving sculptures which expressed their Catholic devotion – but surely most miners were not capable of producing such fine quality pieces of art? Our guide could not answer that one!

Poland's devotion to the Catholic church was also evident in Częstochowa, where we were taken to the Monastery of Jasna Góra to see the precious icon of the Black Madonna (so-called because both the Madonna and the infant Jesus are portrayed with black faces, perhaps deliberately or maybe because of centuries of candle smoke). It is a jewelled wooden icon, supposedly painted by St Luke on a table-top in the home of the Holy Family, brought to Constantinople in 326 AD and from there to Poland – though art experts say it was painted in the 6th or 9th century, and brought to Częstochowa in the 14th century. After reputedly saving the city from Swedish attack in 1655, turning the course of the war, the Black Madonna was declared Queen of Poland, and has been precious to Polish Catholics ever since – many Poles make an annual pilgrimage, often walking 350km (217 miles) over 11 days to reach the monastery. I remember feeling embarrassed to be viewing this image as a tourist, when we were surrounded by crowds of passionate pilgrims: though some of my fellow tour managers pushed closer, I stood silently at a distance, watching as worshippers fell to their knees to approach the icon … some even prostrating themselves flat on the floor in front of it.

Though I was moved to see such devotion in Częstochowa, my strongest emotions were stirred when we visited the site of Auschwitz concentration camp, just outside Krakow. This was a large complex of labour and extermination camps operated by Nazi Germany – at first housing Polish then Soviet PoWs, and later thousands of Roma gypsies. However, it is most infamous for the freight trains which brought Jews from all over Nazi-occupied Europe – an estimated total of 1.3 million prisoners, of whom probably 1.1 million died. Many were never even registered as prisoners, since they were sent straight to the gas chambers when they disembarked from the trains. We visited only Auschwitz I, walking through the gates beneath the cynical slogan 'Arbeit macht frei' (work brings freedom), then between lines of blackened brick buildings (formerly army barracks) – successive extensions of the camp consisted only of wooden huts. The gas chambers and crematoria (where the dead were burned) were destroyed by the Nazis before they retreated as Soviet troops approached, but we saw a reconstruction of one of the crematoria. In the memorial museum were many horrific photographs of prison life and the prisoners themselves (the Nazis often recorded their actions, without any shame), but most moving of all were the displays of prisoners' personal effects – mounds of spectacles, shoes and suitcases, and even hair shaved from their heads to be sold commercially. I had seen photographs before, but to see actual possessions, which had once been touched and used by condemned prisoners … a memory I will not forget. Nor will I forget the face of one of my fellow tour managers (a Jew) as we passed through the gates – his own mother had been imprisoned here and had somehow survived. After this visit, there was nothing more to be said … we drove back to Krakow in silence and spent the night quietly in our rooms, turning over the memories in our minds.

THE BALKANS

ALBANIA

I HAVE VISITED ALBANIA ONLY once, in 1985, when the country was only just opening up after the death, a few months before my visit, of their long-time dictator Enver Hoxha. Tourist facilities were almost non-existent: there were limited hotels... few cafes or restaurants... monotonous food (we ate the same stuffed peppers and fresh grapes at every lunch for two weeks) ... no international airport (we had to fly into neighbouring Yugoslavia) ... and most problematic of all, no trained guides. We started out under the care of a teacher who spoke good English but had no interest in the history or culture of her country – the only information she could provide for us, was the approved 'line' on life in one of the strictest Communist countries in the world (they had broken relations with the Soviet Union in 1961, then even with post-Mao China in 1978, because neither was following the principles of communism strictly enough). She exploded in rage when we spread out to explore instead of sticking close to her, and halfway through the tour she was replaced by a museum curator who had more of the knowledge we craved, but spoke poor English and only slightly better French. However, the difficulties of visiting a country not yet organised for tourism, were far outweighed by the fascination and unexpected beauty of the land.

We were escorted from Titograd (this Yugoslav city only reverted to its ancient name of Podgorica in 1992) by a Yugoslav guide who spent most of the journey warning us that all Albanians were violent troublemakers. So we disembarked with trepidation from our Yugoslav coach at their border control, walking with our luggage to the Albanian customs post, where we were called forward one by one to show our passports and visas. There was no stress, however, and we were even invited into a cool, shady lounge where we could relax while paperwork and baggage checks were completed. Boarding our Albanian coach, we set off along narrow but empty roads – the only traffic was a few trucks, ancient tractors or military vehicles. Private cars were still banned and people travelled by bicycle, horse- or ox-cart, on foot or by hitchhiking ... though our driver had been instructed that he should not stop, to avoid inappropriate contact between us (dangerous?) foreigners and local people. We passed through peaceful villages and fields where people were working in the sunshine. The only slightly disturbing sight amid all this tranquil normality, was the presence at frequent intervals of small, round, concrete gun emplacements, like pale mushrooms sprouting from the earth – no longer used, we were assured, but evidence of a paranoiac fear of outsiders or invasion which had dominated national and international politics until very recently.

On our first full day of sightseeing, we were taken to visit the ancient Schkodra fortress, founded originally in the 4th century BC and enlarged again by 15th century Venetians and 18th century Ottoman Turks. Though there were only ruinous walls to see, I had not expected to find such historic sites in the country – though here I encountered for the first time a quirk of Albania's recorded history: we were told that the original fortress was built by Illyrians, though it was clear that they were talking about the ancient Greeks. Albania was officially at war with Greece from 1940 until they finally re-established diplomatic relations in the 1990s (the state of war was not officially lifted until 2016), and throughout the 40-year rule of the dictator Enver Hoxha, he had tried to reinforce the nationhood of Albania by rewriting history to show them as a distinct nationality and culture since ancient times. It was not appropriate, in his view, that Albanians should be descended from ancient Greeks!

As we drove southwards, I was amazed by the agricultural landscape of the country – I had been regularly travelling in neighbouring Yugoslavia and Greece with my tours and was used to the desolate, waterless 'karst' landscape of the region, where centuries of tree-felling has resulted in the loss of topsoil and exposure of porous limestone rock into which all surface water disappears, leaving land useless for growing crops. Yet here in Albania, we were seeing hillsides neatly terraced and irrigated, producing abundant crops of tobacco, maize, fruit, sugar beet and cotton – the result of the hard work of older schoolchildren and students, who spent one month each year in unpaid labour on national projects like terracing, or even railway building. A huge communal effort, but one which had certainly paid off in terms of the land. Later in our trip, we were woken on a Sunday morning by loudspeakers (located on every street corner in every community) calling the people to 'donate a day to Albania' and join special buses waiting to take volunteers out for a day harvesting cotton or doing other necessary farm work ... and at 6am, crowds were already flocking to the buses.

Everywhere we went, the people were fascinated by us and openly friendly – crowds gathered each time we stopped (despite the efforts of our guides to keep us from all but the official contacts) and several times I was invited into people's homes, if I was walking by myself without the presence of our guide/ guardian. Especially I remember an invitation to visit a home in Korça, where I had broken away from the group (sated with 'official sights') and stopped to photograph a typical house with overhanging upper floors. Two old ladies, dressed in black, approached to speak to me (in broken Italian) and invited me to join them to drink sweet cherry wine in their neat living room.

As we progressed around the country, we were shown magnificent historic sites which were the equal of any major tourist attraction in other lands, yet seemed barely appreciated by the Albanian people and even by our guides. In the city of Durres, we explored the half-excavated 2nd century Roman arena; in Butrint, at the end of a rough track, we were the only tourists visiting the remains of an entire ancient city which flourished both under the Greeks in the 3rd century BC and also under the Romans in the first centuries of the Christian era. Another less well-preserved site was the ancient city of Apollonia, again founded by the ancient Greeks with a grand temple to the god Apollo, developed by the Romans as a major port and later (in the 14th century) the site of an imposing Greek Orthodox church – now lying in ruins but (according to our guide) due for restoration at some time in the future.

Throughout the country we saw a few mosques and many Orthodox chapels and churches, almost all in ruins. Enver Hoxha had tried to ban religion completely and all religious buildings were abandoned in 1968, supposedly with the full agreement of the local people (but then, our officially approved guides would say that!).

Since becoming a Christian when I was just 15 years old, I have been very aware of God watching over me, especially when I have been travelling. In Albania, I experienced this as I broke away from the group one lunchtime, to climb up the hillside to a deserted Orthodox chapel, passing two defensive dogs on the way. As I climbed, I heard the dogs barking again – was someone following me? I reached the chapel, finding it windowless and stripped of all furniture and decoration, but the door was open, so I stepped inside. Within minutes, a young man followed me in, blocking the door with his body as he carefully removed his sunglasses and pushed them into a pocket. He reached for me, so I pretended to grab those sunglasses – clearly they were important to him, so if I threatened to break them, I thought he might leave me alone. That stopped him for a moment, but then he moved forward to pin me against a wall ... so I looked him sternly in the face and declared 'Not in God's house!' A doubtful look crossed his face, but he tried again with a half-smile. I repeated 'Not in God's house!' ... and he stepped back, letting me slip past him out of the doorway to head back down the path. It is good to know that I have divine protection wherever I travel!

Highlights of our sightseeing were the two 'museum cities' which we visited. First we spent a day in Berat, nicknamed 'the town of 1000 windows' because of the wide-windowed houses which climb up its steep hillsides, one on top of the other. We also visited Gjirocastra, called 'the stone city' for its stone-slabbed roofs – I was enchanted by the vine-hung houses, though for our local guide its principal attraction was the (reconstructed) house where Enver Hoxha was born. Outside Tirana (the capital city) we were taken to admire Hoxha's tomb, topped by a massive red marble slab and guarded by three soldiers at all times. Later we were introduced to another Albanian hero – a 15th century prince called Skanderbeg, who fought against Turkish invaders: our coach stopped beside a nondescript modern structure which enclosed a ruined mosque, burial place of this national hero. There was also a huge red Albanian flag featuring a double-headed eagle – Skanderbeg unified north and south Albania in 1444, hence this double-headed eagle on the national flag.

Alongside the historic sites, we were taken to see model schools, farms and factories. Early in our tour we were invited into an exceptionally neat primary school classroom full of well-scrubbed and well-disciplined children who recited patriotic poems to us. The farm we visited, was run as a huge co-operative – most of the crops were sold at subsidised rates in local shops, while any excess (plus cash crops like tobacco and sugar) was sold to the State in exchange for machinery, fertiliser etc. On the other hand, the factory visits were an eye-opener – especially in the precision engineering factory, where any British health & safety officer would have been horrified! We watched as a worker repeatedly extracted blocks of red-hot metal from the furnace, then threw them across the room to another worker – neither wearing any safety goggles. We picked our way across the rough, broken floor, dodging this deadly juggling act and praying for our tour to move swiftly on!

Wherever we travelled in Albania, we found ourselves driving through magnificent scenery of terraced hillsides and forested mountains (which cover 75% of the entire country). Twice we passed the amazingly blue, clear waters of Lake Ohrid (we often retraced our steps, since some roads were considered of inferior quality or ran too close to the sealed Greek border), and finally we descended to the shores of the Adriatic Sea at Saranda, surrounded by groves of olive, lemon and orange trees. I had chosen to visit the country mainly because it was an unusual destination, rather than because I had heard it was especially interesting … yet, against all my expectations, Albania turned out to be a stunningly beautiful country, full of magnificent historic sites and friendly people. I cannot wait to visit again and see how it has developed.

FORMER YUGOSLAVIA

I HARDLY KNOW WHERE TO start with my memories of this region, since it changed so much even during the time when I regularly toured here in the 1970s-80s, and has changed even more in the years since. During the time when I knew it as a tour manager, it was united into one country, Yugoslavia, and I cannot help always thinking of it this way, though the region now comprises 6 different countries plus an autonomous state. Yugoslavia actually only existed as an entity for 73 years in total. From the 14th to 18th centuries, the coastline was mostly under the control of the powerful maritime state of Venice; meanwhile from the 14th to 19th centuries, a large part of the inland territory was under the control of the Muslim Ottoman Turks (though there were periods when Serbia was able to establish an independent Orthodox kingdom); also for centuries, the Catholic Habsburg empire dominated the north-western parts of the region, gradually extending its control southwards until it ruled much of the land. After WW1, the territories formerly belonging to the Habsburgs and Ottomans were drawn together into the kingdom of Yugoslavia, which after WW2 became the communist Federal Republic of Yugoslavia, led by President Tito – an amazing (if autocratic) leader who managed to hold together this fragile union of nations by the strength of his own authority alone. He improved the economy gradually, developing education, industry and tourism, and by 1963 the country was stable enough to allow its citizens considerable freedoms, including foreign travel – many travelled into Germany and Austria as 'guest workers' on special contracts, which allowed them two months holiday each year to return home. I remember the roads being filled with these migrant workers in the summer months, their ancient cars overloaded with consumer goods as they travelled back to their families, then laden with garden produce (especially water melons) when they returned to their workplaces.

When I first visited the country in the late 1970s, I tried to explain its structure to my guests using this simple formula:

- 6 Republics
- 5 Nations
- 4 Languages
- 3 Religions
- 2 Alphabets
- but only 1 Tito

Inevitably, there was no-one powerful enough to succeed Tito when he died in 1980. I was in the country on that day, sitting on the wharf at the port of Split waiting to board a ferry to Italy, and I remember the shockwave which seemed to engulf the people when they heard the news: the ferry sailing was immediately postponed; the customs offices closed; the port workers milled around the docks, some openly crying. The country held together for a few years after his death, but its economy began to crumble and political tensions built up, until in 1991, four republics (Slovenia, Croatia, Bosnia-Hercegovina and Macedonia) declared independence. Serbia and its ally Montenegro opposed that independence, and the Yugoslav Wars began. Slovenia suffered only 10 days of war, perhaps because of the support of their close ally Austria, and Macedonia managed initially to escape attack entirely (though they have since had armed revolts from the Albanian minority living there). However, the two major powers (Croatia and Serbia) plunged into bitter battles, many fought on the territory of Bosnia-Hercegovina – its position at the centre of the region, meant that it had a mixed population including large groups of ethnic Croats and Serbs, so that the war in Bosnia became a civil war, with appalling atrocities committed. In 1995, the combatants were forced by the outside world into a reluctant peace – but when I re-visited in 2018, it was clear that there are still simmering tensions throughout the region. Perhaps we can expect more trouble here in the future?

The first tours I escorted to Yugoslavia, travelled from Hungary for an overnight stop in Zagreb, capital of Croatia. We always seemed to arrive late in to the city, after dragging through the Hungarian border controls and then negotiating narrow country roads where slow-moving hay-carts drawn by oxen, obstructed our passage – especially dangerous as darkness fell, since they carried no lights. This late arrival meant that there was never time for much sightseeing, though our hotel was located close to the historic 14th century church of St Mark, with its stunningly colourful roof covered with complex, elaborate patterns in the tiling. My main memory of this overnight stop is the dinner we were served, our tables spread in a well-spaced horseshoe around a vast dance floor. Our plates were covered with small portions of a wide variety of unrecognisable dishes. None of us had any idea what they were, though there was one small pile which resembled grated cheese, so most guests started with that … only discovering, a few seconds after putting a forkful into their mouths, that it was actually grated horseradish! Our tables were so far apart, that the agonised gasps of one group were not recognised by the next group until they had also swallowed their first forkful.

The driver and I were spared, since we were served last – and on future visits, I was able to warn my guests in advance, to be careful.

As the years passed, I travelled many different routes through Yugoslavia. My only glimpse of the beautiful alpine scenery of Slovenia was during a day-trip from south-eastern Austria to Lake Bled – an excursion which caused some discontent amongst my guests, since certain nationalities (especially South Africans) were not permitted to cross the border and so could not join this trip. However, the excursion was worth any difficulties, since the lake is a sparkling jewel set amidst forested mountains. We cruised across its waters to visit the tiny pilgrimage church perched high on an island, clambering up the long stairway (99 steps) to the viewing terraces. The church is popular for weddings and tradition holds that the groom should carry his bride up the stairway to the terrace, to bring their marriage good luck – if he survives the heart attack, that is!

In the western part of Croatia, some tours stayed overnight at a modern hotel located at the gates of the Plitvice National Park, a vast area of forest rich in wildlife, including brown bear, wolf and lynx. At the heart of the Park is a series of 16 interconnected lakes, separated by ever-changing dams created by algae and sediments which erode from the limestone rock as the water flows from lake to lake, or falls in tall chutes from the cliffs around. We had no time for long hikes into the Park, but before leaving our hotel in the morning, I escorted as many of my guests as were physically able, down a steep concrete path to the shores of one of the largest lakes, then across a precarious walkway of wooden stumps alongside one of the natural dams. At the time, in the 1980s, we were amongst the very few visitors to the Park – we were so privileged to have this natural marvel to ourselves (now it is heavily developed for tourism). In the period when I was bringing groups here, the Yugoslav economy was beginning to collapse, and the value of the Yugoslav dinar was swiftly and dramatically decreasing. Each banknote would become virtually worthless from one visit to the next, so I never tried to carry Yugoslav currency with me between tours. I remember, on one occasion, converting my hard currency into dinars at the hotel reception (since I had to buy entrance tickets to the Park in local currency), and being given such a huge pile of banknotes that I could barely carry them, tottering down the path to the ticket office, desperately hoping that the wind would not catch the pile and blow the money away. By 1990, the government had been forced to revalue their currency, at a rate of 10,000 old dinar to 1 new.

Another route south took me through the town of Banja Luka, where I remember being astounded by the height of its population – both men and women were so tall, that I had to crane my head to look up into their faces. The road continued through the glorious scenery for which this region is famed, following the spectacular gorge of the Vrbas River through thickly forested hills, passing the fortified medieval town of Jajce (once capital of an independent Bosnian kingdom), clinging to the hillside beneath a ruined fortress. Along the roadsides, we passed small outdoor restaurants, each boasting a massive spit outside, where an entire sheep was slowly roasting – though we were always too early in the day for the meat to be ready for us to stop and sample. Instead, our lunch stop was beside the Neretva River in the town of Mostar, famous for its 16th century Ottoman bridge. When I visited in the 1970s, the approach to the bridge was via dark and unsavoury, partially-covered bazaars, where I tried to find a reasonably hygienic stall selling roasted ćevapčići sausages and traditional flat bread for my guests to eat for lunch. When I returned to the city in 2018, I was shocked by the transformation. The bridge was shelled in 1993 by Croat forces (the images broadcast around the world by news services) and destroyed: since it was rebuilt in 2004, it has become a major tourist attraction – the narrow, cobbled streets leading to the bridge are now bright with sunshine, lined with smart cafes and souvenir shops, and packed with tourists. I could see little difference in the reconstructed bridge – even its limestone flooring is still so slippery and polished by passing feet, that it is hard to climb up its shallow steps. However, in the rest of the town, historic mansions and modern apartment blocks are still roofless, with holes blown in their walls (the city was 80% destroyed by shelling). There appears to have been little attempt to rebuild the ruins – instead, new houses have often been built alongside them, or even attached to them. It seems to me that the city is actually proud of these ruins, flaunting them as tourist attractions and revelling in the world-wide attention which they bring.

One Mostar tradition which has been preserved and enhanced for tourists, is diving from the highest point of the bridge into the icy river below. Our guide emphasised for us that it is a dangerous feat, not only because of the height of the bridge (21m/ 69ft) and the depth of the river (5m/ 16ft) but also because he claimed it is one of the coldest flowing rivers in the world: the cardiac shock of suddenly plunging from air temperatures of over 40°C into water with a temperature of only 6°C, could be fatal. I watched several young men preparing themselves for their dives, sluicing themselves with cold water to cool their skin before jumping feet-first into the river. Originally it was done to impress the girls ... now each dive is preceded by lengthy periods of soliciting donations from watching tourists.

Many of our tours followed the spectacular road along Croatia's Adriatic coast, through waterside villages with harbours bobbing with fishing boats and alongside tiny, tempting, shingle beaches – on a hot sunny day, how I wished I could stop to allow my guests to paddle in the crystal-clear water, but the demands of the itinerary meant we had to keep driving. On some tours, we stayed in the fascinating city of Split – location of a heavily fortified, Roman palace built in 305 AD for the emperor Diocletian. Amazingly, the ancient walls are still standing, though over the centuries the Roman buildings inside have been replaced by an entire city of houses and churches, all built in the local, warm yellow limestone. Sightseeing took us on foot alongside the harbour (unfortunately, at the time, bathed in a strong aroma of sewage leaking from the city's poorly maintained infrastructure) to pass through the seaward gate and stroll into a maze of highly polished limestone alleyways. Further south, we crossed the estuary of the River Neretva, dotted with oysterbeds and lined with terraced restaurants, with views out to the Pelješac peninsula. My guests were always fascinated by the sight of the walls climbing across the peninsula around the town of Ston – built in the 15th century and one of the longest defensive walls in the world, originally 7km (almost 4½ miles) long. Another place I would have loved to explore with my guests, but again ... no time! Perhaps one day I will manage to return to the area and visit properly.

Whichever way we travelled into Yugoslavia, our road always led to the unique city of Dubrovnik – the 'Pearl of the Adriatic'. It freed itself from Venetian control in the 14th century and developed into a wealthy, independent maritime state, until it was badly damaged by earthquake in the 17th century and then conquered by Napoleon in the 19th century. It passed into the control of the Habsburg empire, then became part of Croatia – shelled by the Serbs for 7 months in 1991 and badly damaged, but fully restored by the early 2000s. I often tried to approach the city via the road high on the cliffs, so that my guests' first view was a panoramic vista over the entire old town, ringed by immense walls (up to 6m/ 20ft thick on the landward side) which enclose a maze of brilliant red tiled roofs – a communal gasp of excitement always rippled through the coach! When I visited with budget tours in the 1970s, we stayed in a simple hotel in the modern port area, but higher quality tours in the 1980s were booked into the historic Imperial Hotel, still redolent with 19th century grandeur, and located a few steps from the most imposing of the city gates. Some guests rushed straight out to explore the old city, but others seized the chance to relax like Victorian nobility, sipping a cocktail on the elegant verandahs. When I returned to Dubrovnik in 2018, I looked inside this hotel – now part of the Hilton chain, and well beyond my price range!

Sightseeing in Dubrovnik took us across the stone bridge which spans the (now dry) moat around the city, and through the complex of doorways which make up Pile Gate, emerging into an imposing main street, accessible only to pedestrians and lined with gracious mansions built after the earthquake in 1697. The local guide took us from one shady spot to the next (the sun is strong on this coast), telling us stories from the city's glorious past – but, in my opinion, the best way to experience Dubrovnik is simply to wander its alleys and discover its hidden corners for yourself. In 2006, I spent a few days in the city independently, to do just that – especially climbing to the top of the walls to walk right around the city, looking down from the seaward fortifications to the vertical cliffs and violent waves, which were once Dubrovnik's most effective defence. There were already no remaining signs of the serious damage inflicted during the Yugoslav Wars – I could see no difference in the buildings or the atmosphere, from when we used to visit before the siege and bombardment. However, what a shock when I returned to Dubrovnik in August 2018, to find it again under attack – this time sinking under the onslaught of tourism. We had to push against the crowds even to enter through Pile Gate, despite an attempt by local authorities to establish a one-way system to keep inbound and outbound tourists apart. Once inside the walls, it was impossible to get a clear view of any monuments or buildings because of the milling hordes, all shoving and pushing to keep close to their guides. The sun was beating down, the queue for the only public toilet impossibly long ... all the magic and history of this glorious city evaporated into sweaty stress. I adjourned to a cafe outside the walls, happy to pay their exorbitant prices in exchange for a seat and a patch of shade. I was so glad that this was not my one and only chance to explore Dubrovnik!

Despite my 2018 experience, Dubrovnik holds a special place in my heart – perhaps because, during my tour managing years, it was one of the places where I could take a little time for myself, reassured that my guests were safe and happy in their private explorations around the city. On one occasion, I took a ferry across to the island of Lokrum – thickly wooded and surrounded by rocky bathing spots. I made my way to the far end of the island to swim, discovering that the 'beach' there was dedicated to nudist bathing ... oh well, why not? I stripped off and dived from the rocks straight into the cool water – such a delicious sensation on a hot day, to feel the water refreshing every part of my body ... though it was a little painful trying to climb out of the water again, with the waves pushing me repeatedly against the rocks! On another occasion, I took a local bus to the nearby village of Cavtat – a quiet backwater in the 1980s, with just a few pleasant waterside cafes around the harbour. My 2018 tour actually stayed in Cavtat (by now Dubrovnik's hotels have become so expensive, that budget tourism has moved to villages like this) – finding it much more heavily developed for tourism, with restaurants and elegant shops lining the waterfront, but still a peaceful haven compared to Dubrovnik. Here I was able to slip down a purpose-built ladder into the clear, warm water to swim with tourists and local children alike.

On some tours, we stayed long enough in the area to make an excursion into Montenegro, to the magnificent Bay of Kotor – a fjord reaching into the mountains for 30km (18 miles), with its narrowest point just 300m (1000 ft) wide, yet deep enough to take the largest of cruise ships. I first visited the town of Kotor, at the head of the inlet, in the summer of 1980 – after the entire region had been torn apart by an earthquake a year earlier. We parked the coach outside the historic walls which surround the old town, allowing my guests to walk inside – but the town was still virtually abandoned: its population mostly living in tents outside the walls; its houses partly crumbling, with holes in the roofs and cracks in the walls; its streets still littered with rubble. What a transformation when I visited in 2018: now it is a major tourist centre, especially when cruise ships anchor just offshore, and the streets are busy with visitors. It still nestles behind its Venetian walls: narrow alleyways meandering past both Catholic and Orthodox cathedrals; pleasant open squares shaded by trees and patrolled by hundreds of skinny feral cats; slippery stone steps (polished by thousands of feet over the centuries) leading up towards the hilltop fortress. Another huge difference when I visited in 2018 – now there is an international border between Dubrovnik (in Croatia) and Kotor (in Montenegro). The queue of traffic waiting to cross the border was at least three hours long on the main road, and even an hour on the tiny backroad my taxi driver attempted – nearly all German and Austrian tourists, and some visitors from other former Yugoslav states. My recommendation? Do not try to visit this region in high season!

In 2018, we also had time to visit the smaller, but equally historic, port of Perast on the shores of the Bay of Kotor, and to take a boat across to the island of Our Lady of the Rocks. Tradition says that local sailors found an icon of the Madonna on a rock here in the 15th century, and built an artificial island (using wrecked shipping and local stones) around the spot, crowning it with a small chapel dedicated to the Virgin, protector of seamen. Now this church is also a major tourist sight – we had to bob around in the fjord for quite a while before our boatman noticed a spot where he could tie up, hurtling towards the quay before another boat could seize his place. Then we had to queue at the entrance to the church and at every doorway within the building, waiting for space enough to squeeze inside to see the collection of paintings commemorating miraculous rescues at sea, attributed to the Madonna. Perhaps not the best use of an afternoon's time?

In June 1979, I escorted a tour which normally took an overnight ferry from Dubrovnik to Italy – but just a couple of months previously, the region had been devastated by earthquake (killing 150 people) and the port of Dubrovnik was too badly damaged for the ferry to dock. Instead, we had to continue southwards along the coast to the port of Bar, close to the Albanian border. Along the way were sections of cliffside road which had crumbled into the sea, which my driver had to cross on makeshift wooden beams spanning the gap. We made no attempt to drive around the Bay of Kotor, instead taking the small ferry across the narrowest point. Unfortunately, the ramps leading to the ferry were also broken, so the crew tried to position wooden blocks to hold the coach high enough so it did not ground on the broken concrete as we drove on board. As we crossed, one block broke, dropping the coach to the floor, smashing a small motor used for air conditioning – fortunately, on our budget tours, the coach contract did not include air conditioning and we were not using this motor. Finally we crossed the fjord and reached the port of Bar, the only port along this part of the coast still operating – it was packed with desperate travellers! My driver had to force a passage for me through a heaving crowd of potential passengers, so that I could confirm our reservation, though there was no question of being allocated the cabins and 'airline chairs' for which my guests had paid. We were given five six-berth cabins, in the windowless depths of the ferry, with walls running with condensation: I packed as many guests as possible into these, then took the blankets from the cabins for the remainder of my guests who had to sleep on the floors of the lounges. The crossing passed without event ... but then came the disembarkation. I had told my guests to remain inside the ferry until most of the passengers had disembarked, since it was so overloaded that I anticipated a dangerous rush for the gangplanks. I was right! I stood on deck to watch our coach being unloaded, surrounded by travellers desperately forcing their way towards the gangplanks, though they had not yet been opened – such a crush that one of the deck rails actually broke under the pressure. One of the most frightening experiences of my tour managing career – yet I had no complaints from my guests: they were just happy to have arrived safely in Italy.

As the years passed, I found myself often allocated my company's longest tour – a 36-day marathon which traversed the whole of Europe, driving the length of Yugoslavia into Greece, before crossing to Italy and travelling north again. This meant that we drove from Dubrovnik into the Yugoslav state of Macedonia, stopping overnight in its capital Skopje. At first, this was a straightforward route through countryside untouched by tourism – fascinating and beautiful, but also lacking any useful infrastructure: the day's drinks and picnic lunch had to be bought in advance, and my main task was finding a pleasant place to consume them, and a few suitably private spots for 'open-air' toilet stops. As the 1980s progressed, however, tensions were building up in the autonomous Serbian province of Kosovo (through which we had to pass) – by the late 1990s, this exploded into a war, which is still only partially resolved by the presence of NATO troops to enforce peace. When we were travelling through the region, we were warned that there was a threat of kidnapping for ransom, so we were recommended not to regularly use the same road. In one year, I escorted this tour three times, choosing three different routes – often complicated by a lack of signposts to indicate where we should drive. When there were signposts, they were usually only in Serbian Cyrillic script, which I cannot read. On one occasion, we had to stop beside a rural cafe for me to go inside to seek directions – as I approached the counter, I realised that I was the only woman in the building, and the other customers were eyeing me strangely ... fortunately, my driver (a big man) followed me inside when he realised something was not right, and kept me safe as I struggled to get the information I needed, using gestures and a couple of Serbian words I had picked up.

Often this was a long journey, so we only reached Skopje well into the evening – little time for sightseeing, but there was not a lot to see anyway. The settlement thrived under Ottoman rule for 300 years, constructing many mosques, bazaars and hammam baths – but 70% of the city was destroyed by a terrible earthquake in 1963: 16,000 people were initially buried in the ruins and over 1000 died. By the time I was visiting in the 1980s, Skopje had been rebuilt in drab, modernist style with few landmarks – all I remember is the ruined facade of the former railway station, preserved as a memorial, with its massive station clock set permanently at 5.15, the hour when the earthquake struck. The guide on my 2018 tour told me that the Macedonian government has recently spent huge sums on trying to recreate some of the lost architecture of Skopje, as well as a range of avant-garde sculptures – all expensive and heavily criticised by the population ... but the guide was Serbian, and rarely had a good word to say about any of the other former Yugoslav states, so perhaps the city is actually thriving? My 1980s groups spent just one night in a shoddily-built and poorly-maintained hotel: I tried to prepare them for the experience by making a joke about the loose toilets which moved when you sat on them, saying that it was part of an experiment to protect against future earthquakes ... did they get the joke? Or did they take me seriously?

I joined a guided tour in 2018, mainly to revisit some of the parts of former Yugoslavia which I had known 40 years previously – however, we also toured some areas which I had not visited before, especially the inland regions of Montenegro and southern Serbia. Montenegro has to be one of the most scenic countries in Europe – as well as stunning coastal landscapes, its interior is covered with forested mountains. We followed the dramatic rocky Morača Canyon, slashed by the river through limestone ridges which gleam white against cloudless blue skies, the road hollowed out of the precipitous cliffs. However, I was saddened to see Chinese engineers building a new motorway cutting through the mountains in tunnels: this scenic drive will soon be eliminated from tourist itineraries. We stopped to visit Morača Monastery, where two 13th century Orthodox churches lie hidden behind fortifications, suitably dark and mysterious with gloomy green walls and muted frescoes, enlivened only by the sparkling gold of icons. Climbing higher amid forested mountains, we crossed the Crkvina Pass (1060m/ 3500ft), descending through hay meadows and orchards dotted with isolated farms crowned by steep (snow-shedding) roofs, to enter Dormitor National Park. Following the Tara River as it carved its way through a rocky canyon (at 1300m/ 4200ft, one of the deepest in Europe), we drove deeper into the Park to visit Crno Jezero (Black Lake), its deep green water striped with translucent turquoise, ringed by sweet-scented pine forest and backed by rocky peaks – idyllic!

Entering Serbia, we found ourselves in a peaceful rural landscape where each home was surrounded by a thriving vegetable patch and the road was lined with meadows which filled the air with the sweet scent of newly mown hay, all set amid a backdrop of dense forest. Immediately we began to see signs in the Cyrillic alphabet (though here in Western Serbia, there were also some tourist-friendly signs in the Latin alphabet) – in tourism-oriented Montenegro, they have mostly moved over totally to Latin lettering. We spent the night sleeping in the preserved traditional houses of Sirogojno Open-Air Museum, where we were distributed between the small wooden houses nestled amid pine trees, with tiny but enchanting wood-panelled rooms and simple wooden beds. It was a special place to spend the night, especially for the opportunity it gave me to wander into the surrounding countryside early next morning, watching as farmers released their sheep from overnight pens to make their way to the day's grazing, past orchards where the trees were weighed down with an abundance of plums – one farmer noticed my interest, and picked a handful of juicy plums to give to me with a broad smile.

Another border crossing now brought us into the republic of Bosnia-Hercegovina, where immediately we began to see ruined houses (often with a brand-new one next door) – relics of the civil war. What a shock to drive into Sarajevo's crowds and congestion, after Serbia's peaceful rural landscapes … and how strange, after visiting squat, stone-built Orthodox churches, to find elegant Muslim domes and minarets on every corner. The maze of pedestrianised streets which make up the old town were packed with tourists from every part of the world (including many heavily veiled Saudi women), swarming around innumerable stalls selling Bosnian fast-food of fried sausages and flaky pastry pies, with tiny coffee shops offering traditional Turkish-style coffee presented showily on gleaming copper trays. Sightseeing showed us the remains of the original Ottoman city, including a 16th century caravanserai and mosque, then moved into the 19th century Habsburg city, reminiscent of Vienna, built after a terrible fire in 1879 burned through the previously wooden old town. We also saw the simple wall plaque marking the spot where a Serbian assassin took the opportunity to shoot the heir to the Austro-Hungarian empire (Franz Ferdinand) and his wife while they were on an informal visit to the city – the spark which started World War 1.

I was keen to see any relics of the 1974 Winter Olympics, remembering the exploits of our own Torvill and Dean in the ice-dancing competition, but this happy time seems to have been almost forgotten in the city. I ascended the Olympic (Trebevic) Mountain using a cable car which was destroyed in 1995 and completely reconstructed by the Swiss in 2018. There was little to see at the summit, but I found a battered concrete path leading downhill through the forest until eventually it reached the remains of the Olympic bobsleigh track, its concrete banking now defaced with graffiti and its decaying track gradually being reclaimed by nature with moss and small plants rooted in its cracks. Clearly the triumph of this moment in Sarajevo's history has been eclipsed by the horrors which succeeded it – everywhere there were reminders of the siege of Sarajevo, longest in modern history, lasting for almost 4 years (1992-96). Outside the monumental part of Sarajevo, I found dirty, graffiti-covered, crumbling buildings erected in the Communist era – many still pock-marked by the explosion of shells during the war. Exploring the suburbs in search of traditional Ottoman 'mahala' districts with their courtyard houses, I found myself walking through an ancient Islamic cemetery which fell into disuse in 1964, but had to be re-opened for burials during the siege (finally closed again in 2005) – so many tombstones dated from 1996, especially older people in their 60s and 70s (perhaps starved to death?). Despite the fun-loving atmosphere of modern Sarajevo, where streets and cafes are packed with locals and visitors, its terrible story is still all too visible and raw emotions are not far from the surface.

Our journey concluded at Trebinje, located only half an hour from the chaos and hubbub of Dubrovnik, yet a delightfully tranquil town where the streets were empty of all but a few local people. The narrow alleyways of the oldest part of town were still partially enclosed by 17th century walls, while elegant 19th century mansions were built around spacious avenues and parklands outside the walls. In the heat of the afternoon, I walked alongside a clear green river as far as a 16th century bridge, just as elegant as Mostar's (though not as high) but calm and tranquil with no hordes of tourists. As I returned to town, the streets were beginning to buzz with activity as local people emerged to promenade, showing off their partners and babies in time-honoured fashion. Once again, I despair of the tourism industry which has been my life – why does it ruin certain places by packing them to exceed capacity, when there are delightful corners of every country just waiting to be explored?

GREECE

FOLLOWING THE DIFFICULTIES OF TRAVELLING in Yugoslavia, what a relief it always was, to reach the Greek border! After days of struggling to find acceptable refreshment stops and toilet facilities, we had only to drive a few yards from the border post to reach a pleasant roadside restaurant, with clean washrooms and a menu full of familiar and appetising dishes – and with a two hour time change as we crossed the border, it was always lunchtime when we arrived. We were only delayed on one occasion, when one of my guests discovered, as we approached the border, that he had left his passport in the hotel at Skopje. We hurried into the snackbar on the Yugoslav side of the border to beg the use of a phone (no mobiles in those days, of course!) to ring the hotel and arrange for a taxi to bring the document at top speed – fortunately only a 2-hour journey. I waited on the Yugoslav side with my guest, while the driver took the rest of the group across to that pleasant Greek restaurant to wait out the delay.

It was hard to convey to my guests all the information about Greece, which I felt I should give them – it is such an ancient land! Considered 'the cradle of western civilisation', it was already unified into one country in the 4th century BC, expanding into a vast empire reaching as far as India in the 3rd century BC (under Alexander the Great). It was conquered by the Romans, but soon made itself the heart of the Eastern Roman Empire (when the city of Rome fell to barbarians). Eventually it was invaded by the Ottoman Turks in the 15th century, before achieving independence again in 1830 (taking a German prince as its new king). During WW1, Greece became embroiled in a war over Greek settlements which had existed for many centuries in the land which had later become Turkey – the Turkish government attempted to wipe them out in a genocide, but eventually world powers agreed a treaty (in 1923) by which 1½ million ethnic Greeks (followers of the Orthodox faith) were forced out of Turkey and ½ million ethnic Muslim Turks were forced out of Greece. These mass expulsions caused huge problems and, when I visited in the 1980s and 90s, there was still a bitter hatred between the two nations – I had to warn my guests not to refer to the cups of strong black coffee as 'Turkish coffee' but as 'Greek coffee'; 'Turkish delight' was 'Greek delight'; meat on a stick was not 'kebab' (a Turkish word) but rather 'souvlaki'. It took two catastrophic earthquakes in 1999 to soothe the hatred – in August, the Greeks were first to respond with generous aid to a disaster in Turkey ... in September, the Turks responded equally generously to a disaster in Greece. Out of mutual generosity came a considerable easing of political animosity – perhaps a lesson for the rest of the world?

When I was drafted in to help write my company's new brochures (a couple of months' work, each successive year from 1985-95), one of my tasks was to create information booklets on each country we visited – I described Greece as 'the land of sun, sea and mountains', and still today, I cannot think of a better way to describe it. Greece has the 11th longest coastline in the world, with over 200 inhabited islands in both the Ionian and Aegean Seas ... yet the mainland is 80% covered by mountains. On our first day in the country, we travelled down the highway which follows the Aegean coastline, gazing out eastwards over beautiful sandy beaches while to the west were the slopes of Mount Olympus, highest in the country (2900m/ 9570ft) and traditionally considered home of the ancient Greek gods. Finally, we turned into the mountains to one of the most unique places I have ever visited: Meteora Valley, studded with enormous boulders and columns of rock which rise precipitously from the valley floor, many topped with ancient monasteries. Already in the 9th century, Orthodox hermit monks had settled in cracks and fissures in these rocks, and in the 14th century 24 monasteries and nunneries were built, perched on the very summit of these amazing pinnacles – accessed only by ladders or baskets suspended from winches, which could be easily withdrawn if threatened by invading Ottoman Turks. In the 1920s, steps were carved into the rock to access the monasteries which were still functioning, leaving the others to crumble into romantic, inaccessible ruins – when we visited, just four male monasteries and two female nunneries were still operating, often with tiny numbers of monks or nuns.

We drove in our coach along the twisting, precipitous roads which wind among the rocks – such a nerve-racking drive for some of my guests that once, one of them decided she could not stand the terror any longer and so elected to walk several miles back down to our hotel at the foot of the rock pinnacles. Sometimes we stopped only for photographs of the most impressive buildings, but on several occasions we had time to visit one or other of the two largest monasteries (Great Meteora or Varlaam), parking as close as possible, then crossing a modern bridge to reach the long flight of steep, rock-cut steps ascending to the monastery itself. Of course, we could not see much of the interior – that is private to the monks, but we could visit the church and small museum in each of the monasteries, and see the winch-house where provisions are still hauled up using rope and net. We stayed in a lovely hotel close to the rock pillars, equipped even with a small swimming pool, and in the evenings I would gather my guests around the pool in the warm twilight hours, sipping wine as we listened to the echoing sound of the huge drums used by each monastery to call their brothers, and the few hermit monks still living in nearby caves, to worship. A wonderful, evocative sound which lingers in my memory.

The mountainous nature of much of the Greek mainland, means that there are few roads to choose when travelling south through the country, so from Meteora we were obliged to return to the coastal highway, driving through the Pass of Thermopylae – a narrow passage which historically was the only easy route from northern to southern Greece. Here I had the chance to tell my guests one of the many legends of ancient Greece – the story of the heroism of King Leonidas and his 300 Spartans who held off an army of (perhaps) 1 million invading Persians in 480 BC, giving the rest of the Greek army time to retreat in good order. Legend tells that they might have resisted indefinitely, except for the treachery of a local shepherd who told the Persians of a small mountain path, which allowed them to outflank the Spartans and then to slaughter them to the last man – except, of course, the one who survived to tell the heroic tale! Further south, we encountered an even more famous legend from Greek history, as we passed the plain of Marathon: here a battle was fought by the heavily outnumbered Athenians against the Persians in 490 BC, this time producing a resounding victory. A herald was sent to run from Marathon to inform the nervously waiting Athenians of the victory, supposedly gasping the single word 'Victory' before collapsing and dying of exhaustion – I expressed that to my guests with a loudly grunted 'Ugh!' on the microphone, which always caused a ripple of laughter. When the first modern Olympics were being planned in 1896, the organisers were seeking an event which would reflect the glory of ancient Greece – they chose to recreate this legend, originally racing for 40km/ 25 miles (the distance from Marathon to Athens), though today the marathon event has been fixed at 42km (just over 26 miles).

Before reaching Athens, most of my tours made one more excursion into the mountains – this time to the foothills of Mount Parnassus and the ruined temples of Delphi. In ancient times, this site was home to one of the most respected, sacred oracles in the classical world. Many great leaders consulted the priestess who was supposedly possessed by the spirit of the god Apollo, producing incomprehensible ravings which were interpreted by the temple priests into poetic phrases – many of them famously ambiguous. King Croesus asked if he should attack the Persians and was told that 'he would destroy a great empire' if he did – his attack failed, and it was his own empire that was destroyed. The Roman emperor Nero was told 'the number 73 marks the hour of your downfall' – he assumed that meant he would rule until he was 73 years old, but in fact he was quickly deposed by a 73-year-old nobleman, Galba. My guests were fascinated by stories about the Oracle of Delphi, but their visit to the archaeological site was less impressive – the temple was abandoned when Christianity came to Greece, and the area was partly buried by landslide and earthquake over the centuries. Excavations started in 1893, but there was still little for us to see except the foundations of walls and a few broken columns. My guests gamely followed the guide up the extremely steep Sacred Way, usually managing to reach the ruins of the Temple of Apollo … but it was always so hot at this site, and the ruins allowed for little shade. Most guests gave up at this point, choosing to sit on a rock and admire the amazing views over the vast olive groves filling the valley far below, whilst only the most dedicated continued further up the steep slope to reach the ancient Theatre, gratefully collapsing on to the rings of stone seating cut into the hillside, to admire the view from this higher vantage point.

Though most guests did not appreciate the ruins of Delphi, we all enjoyed its magnificent rural situation, calm and peaceful despite the many tourist groups plodding across the ancient stones, the air warm and scented with wild thyme from the hills around … such a contrast from our next destination, Athens! Sadly, my memories of this historic city are tainted by the difficulties of managing a tour group here – the roads were jammed with traffic, so that we wasted much of our time simply moving from one attraction to the next; the air was thick with pollution, worsened by the airless heat of a Greek summer. The principal sight included in our city tour was the Acropolis Hill and the Parthenon Temple on its summit, but climbing the hill meant steep steps made of dangerously slippery marble, impossible for the less athletic of my guests, meaning that they missed out on the main highlight of their city visit. Even those who managed to reach the cluster of temples at the top, discovered that they could barely hear the commentary of their local guide, because there were so many other groups fighting to stand close to each of the buildings, their guides shouting commentary in multiple different languages. Perhaps today, with the invention of discreet wifi microphones and individual earpieces for each group member, visitors are better able to absorb the history and atmosphere of the Acropolis? For me, the most pleasant part of our visits to Athens were the cooler evenings, when we strolled into the narrow streets of the Plaka district for a tasty dinner of Greek specialities washed down with pine-flavoured retsina wine, serenaded by local musicians – when suitably lubricated by smooth 'ouzo' aperitif, my guests were able to finally relax and even join local dancers swinging around the tables in elongated Syrtaki lines.

My company's hotels in Athens were often modern buildings located on the busy main highways of the city, but on one occasion we were lodged in a hotel overlooking a dusty garden and the columns of the Temple of Olympian Zeus. A beautiful view from our windows, but made especially memorable because we were there during the Greek Easter festival (on a different date from Easter in Britain, because the Orthodox faith uses a different calendar from the western church). On the evening of Good Friday, the bells of a tiny chapel in the garden opposite our hotel began to ring, continuing their mournful tolling throughout the night and the next day. Finally, as midnight approached and Easter Day started, crowds of worshippers gathered around the chapel, each carrying an unlit candle. On the stroke of midnight, the doors of the chapel opened and a priest appeared, carrying a flame, which he used to light the candles of those nearest to him. Gradually each person's candle was lit by their neighbour, as the crowd sang Easter hymns – when all were lit, and the priest had proclaimed a blessing, the crowd moved off, their candles carrying twinkling light in every direction into the dark night. An unforgettable and moving sight!

My first visit to Athens was with a friend in 1978, free from the constraints of being part of a group, still young and enthusiastic about exploring new places – but even then, I was not impressed with the city. The airport road was lined with half-built houses and shops, open building sites and huge lurid advertisements, though it eventually changed to elegant, tree-shaded avenues lined with the mansions which housed embassies and government offices. We left the airport bus in Syntagma (Constitution) Square, with its classical Parliament building guarded by 'evzone' soldiers (tall and muscular, though dressed in tights and pom-pom shoes) and set off to find accommodation (armed with my copy of 'Europe on 10$ a day'), dragging our luggage through the streets to an address recommended in the book. We both were finding Athens too noisy and crowded, but felt that we ought at least to see the city since we were there, so we booked a city tour – spending the first hour touring almost every street in central Athens, squeezing down narrow, traffic-choked streets lined with shops which seemed to have more goods outside on the pavements or hanging above the door, than they had indoors. It was a good introduction to Athenian life, though we were actually just picking up guests from a range of hotels, and eventually we returned to our starting point to join the proper tour – passing the Parliament, driving through shopping streets to Omonia Square and then up to the Acropolis. We trudged upwards alongside thousands of other tourists, including uniformed schoolchildren arriving by the bus-load from a cruise ship. The best part of the tour was when we continued up a narrow winding road through olive and cypress groves to Kaissariani Monastery, lying peacefully among the trees, infested with hundreds of feral cats which were now the sole occupants of the buildings.

On this first visit to Athens, my friend and I arrived by air – the airport was packed, so we had to suffer long queues to reach passport control then again at customs, finally discovering that Greek bureaucracy ordained that only one exit door was available to the outside world: we popped out like corks from a bottle. Later, as a tour manager, some of my tours also arrived in Greece by plane – the airport was always crowded with tourists in the summer, which made it difficult to keep track of my group amongst the crowds. I will not forget one occasion when my guests had scattered all over the terminal to complete paperwork, and I had to collect them together again for a group check-in. By now, we had been together for many weeks and my guests were used to hearing me yodel loudly when I needed to catch their attention – the sound of a full-volume yodel was not familiar to the other travellers in Athens airport, however, so the entire terminal froze into shocked silence at the sound, allowing my guests to move swiftly towards me.

On every tour I conducted, our stay in Athens included a cruise to several Greek islands. Sometimes it was just a day cruise to three nearby islands in the Saronic Gulf – I found Hydra the most attractive, with a picturesque harbour and white-painted houses climbing the hillsides from the shore. More often, we set off for a 3-day or 4-day cruise across the Aegean Sea to visit Kusadasi in Turkey (for the chance to visit the ancient Greek settlement of Ephesus, or else to bargain for carpets and copperware in the bazaar); Heraklion in Crete (to visit the archaeological site of Knossos); the magnificent island of Santorini, its white-painted village perched on the vertical sides of an ancient flooded volcanic crater; and brief visits to Mykonos and Patmos – the longer itinerary also included a day in Rhodes. I must admit that I often did not join my guests on their sightseeing visits from the ship – instead seizing the chance for some rest and recuperation, in the midst of a tour where I was on duty continuously for over a month. However, on my 1978 visit, my friend and I quickly left the hubbub of Athens and adjourned to the islands for a couple of weeks.

We booked ourselves on to the first ferry to depart from the port of Piraeus (destination Mykonos), pushed on and on by the crew as we boarded, till we reached the very back of the vessel, open to wind and weather ... our tickets were only for Deck Class. Our travelling companions were a very mixed bunch – a sprinkling of Americans and Australians with backpacks, a huge Greek lady and her diminutive friend (she determined that our bench was the only suitable seat for her and wriggled herself into place, but at least her bulk kept us warm). Also near us was a Greek family – Mama and friend, Papa, demure little daughter and a terror of a young son who delighted in doing everything his father forbade, especially when he joined forces with another little terror from another family. Our first sight of the islands was barren and forbidding, with no sign of house, animal or even grass ... until finally we reached some of the inhabited islands – most notably Tinos: a pilgrimage island where many Greeks (including our huge lady) were coming to seek healing from a miraculous icon.

As we left Tinos, the sun became hotter, so we moved up to the top deck for our first magical glimpse of Mykonos – its town a sparkling jumble of square white houses, facing on to a charming fishing harbour full of little boats bobbing on the water. We were delighted – at last the scenery we had been hoping for, and sunshine to go with it! As the ferry tied up and we all scrambled to disembark, we were met by hordes of toothless old men and black-clad women, crowding around the gangplank calling 'Rooms! Rooms!'. We had nothing pre-booked, so we allowed ourselves to be shepherded to one side by a pleasant-looking, middle-aged woman in black, who spoke excellent English. When she had made sure that she could find no more customers from the passengers, we set off for her house, making our way right around the harbour, then disappearing into the maze of twisting alleyways which make up the main part of the town. At last, we were there – one of a pair of typical whitewashed square houses facing a large stone-flagged plaza. Our door was reached by a few steps, so we had a tiny private verandah outside our door, with potted plants and space for two chairs. The shower and toilet were up a flight of outside stairs on the side of the building, but this (and lumpy mattresses) was the only problem.

Our holiday was all about resting and relaxing, so we spent most of our days on Mykonos on the coarse sand beaches, leaving only to seek a cheap meal in one of the waterfront cafes – most days, that meant either Greek salad or stuffed vegetables at the Pelican Restaurant: named after Petros, the pelican adopted by the fishermen of Mykonos and so famous that he even had a (differently coloured) understudy, so that every tourist had the chance to see him. The two birds never appeared together, so it was confusing to find him 'shifting colour' from white to pink! Most days, as we took a leisurely breakfast in the Pelican, we would watch cruise ships anchoring offshore – laughing (with the cruelty of youth!) at the indignities the immaculately-clad cruisers had to suffer to get ashore, packed like sardines into cramped shuttle boats. When cruise ships (usually 4 or 5 at a time) were in port, the island bustled with life – tourists buying bags, woolly hats, woolly jumpers ... they considerably reduced the stocks of goods in the shops, and all next day the streets were filled with the clatter of knitting needles as women worked to replenish supplies. We were in no hurry, watching the bustle around us as we sipped our cups of Nescafé (provided specially for tourists who did not like the strong Greek coffee). As the cruisers returned to their ships, we ambled homewards, stopping to investigate the sound of loud Greek music in an informal club. Clearly the owner was offering free drink to any locals who would come and perform Greek dances for us – their strained, self-conscious first attempts became freer and more enthusiastic as the evening progressed and the drink flowed. More and more Greeks leapt up to dance to impress their tourist girlfriends, and finally we found ourselves dancing too – finally lurching home, narrowly missing the patrolling tourist police. Well ... I guess you were once young, too?

On overcast days, we explored the island – hitching rides with local truck drivers from village to village. One day we took the boat to Delos, Island of Apollo, chugging out into fairly choppy seas. We had no idea of what we were going to see (and did not really care – we just wanted an excursion), so we were quite amazed as we arrived in the tiny anchorage and saw masses of ruins stretching along the shore and up the hill, with occasional marble columns rising out of the maze of dry-stone walling. We disembarked and paid our 50-drachma entry fee, then decided to turn in the opposite direction from most of the tourists, avoiding the rock-cut stairs which ascend the Sacred

Mountain, to lose ourselves in a maze of ruined chambers – now alive with every size of lizard scuttling between the stones. Just what had all these ruins been? There was no-one to tell us, and (in 1978) no internet to search.

After some days, we decided to move on, taking the overnight ferry to Rhodes. We found some reasonably comfortable plastic benches up on the boat deck (we were travelling deck class again) by the 3rd class coffee bar, and settled in for the night – looking like a couple of tramps, wrapped in all the clothing we possessed in order to keep warm, since we had no sleeping bags. First stop in the early hours of the morning was the isle of Patmos – a lovely peaceful little harbour with a few fishing boats rocking on their moorings, and just a couple of lights showing on a village street stretching away up the hill ... otherwise all asleep. Then on fairly quickly to Leros, where I think the local football team must have been coming home – the quay was packed with cheering and chanting people (even at 3am!) and the first man off was chaired and paraded along the quay. Next stop, Kalimnos: I slept through this one, but two acquaintances got off there – an American couple who had sold their home and all their possessions to travel the world. We later met them in Rhodes – very dispirited and dejected, wondering where to go next to escape the winter. Last stop before ours was Kos, where we heard the first threatening rumblings of thunder – as we pulled away from the island, we plunged into the heart of a terrific thunderstorm which followed us for four hours, all the way to Rhodes. We passed through thick clouds of torrential rain, lit with an eerie red glow by the sun behind them, though between clouds we caught tantalising glimpses of the high barren cliffs of Turkey with occasional white mosques on the hillsides. The worst rain came just as we sailed into the harbour of Rhodes at 11am, with water pouring from one side of the deck to the other in great waves as the ship rolled – what an introduction to the Isle of the Sun!

As we got off the ferry, we accepted the offer of accommodation in a simple hotel in the city, rejoicing to find hot water and a bath attached to our room. First stop next day was the cycle-hire shop, wavering our way off through the streets of Rhodes, trying desperately to get used to back-pedalling brakes and to cope with local traffic at the same time (the rule seemed to be 'bikes never have right of way'). We cycled through miles of hills covered by fragrant pine woods, catching occasional glimpses of beautiful rocky coves and isolated modern hotels, returning to spend the evening among the fragrant gardens of the Son et Lumiere show. We were part of an audience of only around 10 people, sitting in a large arena surrounded by huge bushes of sweet-smelling roses and trees which closed us off from present-day Rhodes, while we were transported back to the time of the Turkish capture of the city by means of taped dialogue and music, combined with lights playing on the fortifications above us. That inspired us, next day, to explore the historic city centre, including the Knight's Quarter, with the famous Street of Knights lined with the residences of the various nationalities ('tongues') of knights – now these palaces were private homes, though very run-down. Nearby were huge areas of very decrepit old houses, some in ruins and yet with people still living in the cellars or in wooden huts among the broken walls. The narrow streets and alleyways were crossed by arches holding up the buildings on each side, and all along the roadsides were tiny, very dark shops and bakeries which looked especially unhygienic, with ovens at the back and all the tools of baking lying on the floor. The bread looked and smelled appetising but was heaped unwrapped on tables, for flies and cats to have free access.

Rhodes Town had not impressed us, and the weather did not help – it poured with rain all night and was still drizzling as we returned our bikes and debated what to do with the rest of our stay. We decided to hitch-hike to Lindos, quickly getting a lift in a little lorry so heavily laden it could barely manage the hills – but it took us into the sunshine, through wild and rocky scenery covered with olives, vines and orange trees, and with occasional glimpses of lovely bays below high cliffs. The lorry dropped us just before Lindos, but after a few minutes, an empty coach stopped (without even being asked) and picked us up … in 1978, it was still possible for young girls to accept lifts without fear! Lindos was enchanting – a beautiful, well-enclosed bay and sandy beach, with lines of white houses clustered along narrow rough streets, all overlooked by the towering acropolis. After a quick swim, we decided to take a traditional donkey-ride up to the acropolis – unfortunately, my donkey kept leaning against walls or walking on the very edge of the path (above a precipitous drop)! After a delightful day, we did not want to risk waiting for the last bus home, so decided to try hitch-hiking again, this time offered a lift in a van with three Greeks and their load of sponges. We sat in the back on sacks of sponges, chatting to one of the men, a volatile Greek called Petros, who told us he had been a sponge diver for 20 years, diving up to 40 metres (130ft) deep.

We enjoyed Lindos so much, that we decided to spend the last days of our holiday in the village – rushing to the bus station next morning to try to get a seat on one of the crowded local buses. There were hundreds of people queuing, and a huge surge of them jammed the first bus to arrive. Then a second bus arrived and I was ideally positioned, able to grab the front seats. Unfortunately, the conductor tried to put us off on to Bus 3 because he did not want to load our luggage in the boot and it was not allowed inside ... but I played stupid and eventually he gave up, stowing our bags underneath. Then we were off, passing through villages made up of rather ramshackle, one-storey homes, populated by crowds of women in thick double boots (to protect against snake-bite) and white headscarves, and groups of men drinking coffee in the bars. We passed vineyards and groves of olive or orange trees, over dried-up watercourses, and once along a raised roadway through a swamp.

In Lindos, we accepted the offer of a little, black-clad lady for a room in her house – with a pine door, pine window-frames, pine ceiling and pine bed, so it smelled delightfully fresh! Outside our window was the route up to the acropolis for donkeys, so all day we could hear the clatter of hooves and shrieks of terrified tourists hanging on for grim death and trying to look dignified at the same time. After a short visit to the beach, we strolled around the town and the nearby rocky landscape – heavily eroded into caves and clefts, used by the local people as shelters for their donkeys, goats and chickens, setting up stools to milk the goats among the rocks. For meals, there was only one (packed) restaurant still open (it was November), but the food and service were excellent ... and so cheap! Finally, we could afford to sample the famous Greek lamb, and next day the swordfish. The last full day of our holiday was an idyll of sunshine and blue skies, soft sandy beach and warm sea, before the weather again turned to torrential rain as we boarded the bus back to Rhodes to start our journey home. This early bus turned out to be the school bus and, since it was Greek National Day, some children were in national dress of blue silk pantaloons and red jackets over lacy white blouses – one last wonderful memory from my first visit to Greece.

As a tour manager in the 1980s and 90s, my tours continued from Athens towards Patras, to take a ferry across the Adriatic to Italy. The direct route was a monotonous highway, though it crossed one of the wonders of the modern world – the Corinth Canal. It was originally planned in the 1st century AD, and the Roman emperor Nero even broke the first soil personally, but the plan was abandoned after Nero's death, and not revived until 1881. Even then, it was an incredibly difficult and expensive task to cut through 4 miles of rock, linking the Aegean and Ionian Seas – the original builders went bankrupt, and later owners have never made an economic success of the canal: it is too narrow for most modern shipping and subject to vicious tides entering from the two different seas. I never saw anything but a few pleasure craft using the canal – but my guests were able to take dramatic photographs from the bridge which spans the waterway, 45m (148ft) below.

Occasionally, I escorted a tour which took a more roundabout route to Patras, visiting the ancient site of Olympia along the way. My guests (almost exclusively Australians and New Zealanders on these very long tours, and mostly passionate about sport) were excited to visit the location of the original Olympic Games (held every 4 years from the 8th century BC until 393 AD, when they were banned by the Roman emperor), when athletes from all parts of the Greek world, and later from the entire Roman empire, competed in honour of Zeus, king of the Greek gods, and his wife Hera. Once there were over 70 temples on the site, as well as the Stadium (the running track), Hippodrome (for chariot racing), Palaestra (for boxing and wrestling) and other sporting facilities. Sadly, repeated flooding from rivers and tsunamis, as well as earthquakes, destroyed most of these buildings over the centuries – all my guests could see was a large site full of trees and green spaces, with occasional fragments of walls and colonnades. Most impressive was the passage leading into the Stadium, where we walked between 2m (6ft) high walls of massive stone blocks and beneath a reconstructed archway … to find nothing more than an open space surrounded by grassy banks where there were once seats. Altogether, an underwhelming experience! Yet this site is still the place where the modern Olympic flame is lit from sunlight reflecting in a mirror in front of the ruined Temple of Hera, before being carefully transported as a torch to the country hosting the Olympics – so it still makes a meaningful and relevant visit. It was not easy to reach by coach, however – we followed a route marked as a main road on the map, to find ourselves squeezing through tiny villages where the road was overhung by the projecting upper storeys of houses. In several places, I had to descend from our (extra-high-deck) coach and guide the driver cautiously around these obstacles, wondering all the time whether we would eventually reach a bend which we could not negotiate. Fortunately that did not happen – I do not think he could have reversed back along that road!

Our final sight of Greece was always the port of Patras – a bustling and business-like port, filled with freighters and ferries to all the Ionian islands and various Italian ports. After the comfort of our Greek Island cruise, the ferry was a shock to the system. My guests were accommodated in cabins, but located in the bowels of the ship, constantly humming from the vibrations of the engines. The lounges were basic, with plastic benches for seating and stained carpet on the floors, whilst the restaurant was a series of self-service hatches. Though officially, diners could choose when to eat within a two hour period, I had to warn my guests to queue up to be among the first to be served, since often the most popular dishes quickly ran out, and sometimes there was no food available at all after the first hour or so. On one memorable tour, I was working with a particularly difficult driver – he was refusing to complete all his required duties, and I had been obliged to have strong words with him before leaving Athens. In response, he tried to undermine me by gathering a small group of guests around him, telling them that he knew better ... they did not need to queue, but instead could join him in the ship's bar to wait until the queues had dispersed. Inevitably, they found that there was no food left for them – they learned the hard way, that I DID know what I was talking about, and that it was best that they followed my suggestions in future. Thankfully, it was rare to have tensions like this in my groups – usually we managed to mould ourselves into a friendly 'family' for the duration of the tour, and my driver was almost always a vital and supportive ally.

CONCLUSION

AS I HAVE BEEN WRITING this memoir, I have become increasingly aware of how much Europe has changed over the decades since I first started exploring the continent. Even during my career as a tour manager, I noticed many changes developing in the countries I was visiting, and in the ensuing years there have been even greater transformations – most notably the collapse of the Soviet bloc in 1989/90, when countries formerly lumped together as 'Eastern Europe' and hidden from easy view behind the Iron Curtain, suddenly emerged again as individual countries with their own culture and history. Now they are considered to be 'Central Europe', whilst the former republics of the Soviet Union have become the 'Far East' of the continent. During the 1970s and 80s, I often visited Yugoslavia – but a vicious war in the 1990s tore that country into 6 separate states, with another still struggling for full independence. On the other hand, for most of my career as a tour manager there were two Germanys – I was privileged to celebrate their reunification, both as a visitor and through the experience of a friend living in the former East.

The tourist industry in which I was involved for so many years, has also been transformed. Numbers of visitors have soared, especially as countries like Chile, India and most notably China, have boomed financially, allowing their citizens to travel ever further afield. In response, the tourist industry has become more tightly regulated, bringing limitations to what visitors can see and do – though entrepreneurs have also opened new opportunities, too. Over the years there have been many improvements which have eased the task of today's tour managers and the comfort of their guests – mobile phones and the internet; wifi microphones; en-suite hotel rooms; air-conditioned coaches. All of these developments have certainly been greatly appreciated ... but I am glad to have been a tour manager in an age when I was less restricted, both by local authorities and also by my company itself; when I was free to diverge from the official itinerary (without fear of litigation) to show my guests lesser-known corners, which I had discovered for myself during off-season private visits.

I am sure that many countries have again changed beyond recognition in the years since I last visited. Writing this book has made me realise that I can no longer claim to know Europe well ... it is time to get travelling again!

ALSO BY THE AUTHOR

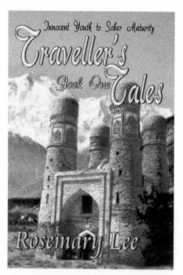

Traveller's Tales: Innocent Youth to Sober Maturity

Traveller's Tales: Advancing Years Will Not Stop Me!

ACKNOWLEDGEMENTS

I DID NOT INTEND TO write this book. Long ago, I had disposed of the notes I made during my career as a tour manager, and it was many years since I had thought about my travels around Europe, concentrating instead on visits to much further-flung parts of the world (described in my two-part book *'Traveller's Tales'*). So I am grateful to those who convinced me to start trawling again through my memories, to see what emerged – especially to my brother and sister-in-law Chris and Jenny Lee, who were sure that there was another book in me!

Once I started to write, I was amazed how many stories resurfaced; they were not forgotten after all, only pushed behind more recent experiences ... but would they be of any interest to others? Many thanks are due to those who volunteered to read some of the chapters to answer that question – especially Jan Bates, Gill and Hans Weghofer, Carina Rogers, Mary Kerslake and Gloria McBean: your criticisms were greatly appreciated, and your encouragement hugely valued.

I am also grateful to Mirador Publishing – especially my editor Sarah, for her encouragement to go ahead and publish this volume, and her patience in guiding me once again through all the technicalities of publication.

Again, I am grateful to Cath d'Alton for producing clear and informative maps to escort my readers as we travel together around Europe.

Most of all, eternal thanks are due to my God, who has constantly watched over my travels throughout the decades, protecting me and smoothing my path – Praise Him!

Lightning Source UK Ltd.
Milton Keynes UK
UKHW011143160621
385610UK00001B/5